DI025467

LIFE CHANGES

**GROWING
THROUGH
PERSONAL
TRANSITIONS**

SABINA A.
SPENCER ◆ ADAMS
JOHN D.

Impact 🖐 *Publishers*
Post Office Box 1094
San Luis Obispo, California 93406

Library of Congress Cataloging-in-Publication Data

Spencer, Sabina A., 1951 -
    Life changes: growing through personal transitions / Sabina
A. Spencer and John D. Adams.
        p.   cm.
    Includes bibliographical references.
    ISBN 0-915166-68-2
    1. Life change events.   2. Life change events — Problems,
exercises, etc.   I. Adams, John D., 1942 -   . II. Title.
BF637.L53S64   1990
155.9 — dc20   90-4246
                                                              CIP

PUBLISHER'S NOTE
This publication is designed to provide accurate and authoritative information in regard to the subject matter covered. It is sold with the understanding that the publisher is not engaged in rendering psychological, medical, or other professional services. If expert assistance or counseling is needed, the services of a competent professional should be sought.

Cover design by Sharon Schnare, San Luis Obispo, California

Printed in the United States of America

Published by *Impact* 🐚 *Publishers*
POST OFFICE BOX 1094
SAN LUIS OBISPO, CALIFORNIA 93406

CONTENTS

ACKNOWLEDGEMENTS

This book has grown out of the many changes, chosen and otherwise, that we have been through in our lives and accounts our workshop participants have shared with us. Our own experiences have included marriage, divorce, job loss, deaths of parents and friends, moves to other countries, career shifts, and many more.

Naming all the people who have loved and guided us through these challenging times would necessitate a book in itself. However there are some that we must give special mention: Bill Paul, Sherman Kingsbury, Pam Allsop, Donald Wolfe, Herb Shepard, Dani Monroe, Bob Tannenbaum, "By" Barnes, Juanita Brown, Don Land, Jim and Linda Crites, Graham Pratt, Pir Vilayat Inayat Khan, Robert Fritz, David Nurenberg, Barbara Sloan, Jit Chopra, Linda Ackerman-Anderson, Jack and Louise Hawley, Bhagavan Sri Sathya Sai Baba, Bernie Wetzel, Sarah Summers and Paul Haddock. Each was a central figure in the life of one or both of as we were making major transitions.

We also want to acknowledge contributions to our life change curve by Barrie Hopson and John Hayes, both of Leeds, England. In the early 1970's, John Adams, Barrie Hopson and John Hayes co-authored a book called *Transition: Understanding and Managing Personal Change*. The book was written for the academic and professional market, and it developed a generic model for describing transitions.

The studies by the Menninger Foundation in the 1960's on Peace Corps trainees' adjustment and experiences, and the work of Elizabeth Kubler Ross on death and dying, both provided a rich research base for our work on change and transitions.

Special thanks also to Ginger Swain for developing the "Letting Go" ritual we adapted in Chapter Seven; and Göran Wiklund and Roger Benson for their ideas on the "Should Line" and the "Spirit Curve."

Finally we were delighted to have discovered Impact Publishers. Bob Alberti and his colleagues were exceptionally supportive as this book came to life. It has really been a pleasure to work with them every step of the way. We would especially like to thank Bob for providing us with excellent ideas to enrich the manuscript, and Sharon Skinner for her patience and attention to detail in bringing the book to print.

Sabina A. Spencer
John D. Adams
Winchester, Virginia
April, 1990

DEDICATION

*With love
to Priscilla and Paul,
Lyman and Ruth;
and to all our "family"
throughout this wonderful world!*

To Lucille,

With our very best
wishes for a healthy life,

Warmly Salina + John

PART ONE

LIFE CHANGES
AND
THE NATURE OF
PESONAL TRANSITION

──────────────────────── **1**

LIFE CHANGES

Have you ever found yourself wandering in a daze as if you'd
been hit on the head with a two-by-four? Have you awakened
in the morning wondering if you'll ever be "normal" again?

Do you remember days when you went to work feeling as
if you didn't want to be there, being bothered by the silliest
little things for no apparent reason? Maybe you've even found
yourself questioning whether life was really worth living?

Did you ever lie in bed at night unable to sleep, watching
the patterns on the ceiling and wondering if you were going
crazy — so confused about what you *really* wanted from your
life, your job, your relationships that you didn't know if you
were coming or going?

If you answered "yes" to any of these questions you've
probably experienced the trials and triumphs that come with
life's major changes. We intend this book to be a helpful guide
or roadmap for you and for others who travel through these
very natural — yet often bumpy — times in life.

Why We Wrote The Book

Wherever we go these days, we run into people talking about divorce, loss of a job, a new marriage, the death of a loved one, a relocation, retirement, or others of life's many changes. It seems that just about everybody is either just beginning a change, right in the middle of one, or just finishing one, and wondering how long it will be before they have to start all over again.

For most of us, change is not something that happens now and again. It seems to have become "a way of life." Just as we think things are "back to normal," we come face to face with the next change. Stability seems to be a thing of the past, something we only get to dream about.

By examining our own experiences and those of many hundreds of our workshop participants, we've found a predictable and quite natural sequence of adjustment that people go through when they make any kind of change. When people find that their experience is normal, they become less afraid and more aware of the learning that comes from the ups and downs of the transition process.

Today people want to make the most of the changes they face, whether they're changes they've chosen or ones that come out of the blue. There is willingness to prepare for the consequences that follow a major change, rather than leaving it all to chance. Still, no matter how much preparation you do, you can't always avoid the "emotional hiccupping" that comes with life's bigger changes. This book is designed to help you come to terms with this part of the change, and to enhance your experience of transition with more growth and less pain.

Interestingly, we have found that even if the change is positive or chosen — such as getting married or taking a new job — you are as likely to experience the same seven stages of transition as when negative change has been imposed on you by someone else — such as being left by a spouse or being fired.

This means that even such positive changes as having a baby, finding your "soul-mate," or moving to a desirable part of the country may trigger intense feelings and thoughts that come as a complete surprise.

It is often harder to understand the downside of wanted changes, because you're expecting that everything's going to be "wonderful" and you'll live happily ever after. For example, getting married might be great, but you'll probably have to go through the process of "divorcing your singleness" — and that can be upsetting.

How much the transition "hurts" depends a lot on how much you are taken by surprise or shocked by the change. It is often the novelty of a situation that deepens the experience. There are other factors that influence how intensely you are aware of the transition stage; we'll talk about them in Chapter Three.

In the past, change has been seen more as an "event" and not as a "process." Once the event has happened, people are expected to get on with their lives as quickly as possible and get back to "normal." Reality, however, is very different. Whatever the change is, in order to have something new in our lives we have to let go of "the way things used to be" — and that takes time.

It sounds simple but few of us have been taught how to cope with the emotional confusion that comes with grieving the old situation while preparing to face the new one. It's this process of adjusting to an important life change that we'll be taking you through.

Whether the change is one you have chosen or one you wish would go away, the transition forces you to leave the known and step into the new and unknown territory. William Bridges (1980) describes these phases as endings, neutral zone, and beginnings.

Whether you are thinking about making a change or are slap-bang in the middle of one, we want this book to become your valuable companion. It is designed to help you under-stand what is happening as you journey on "the roller coaster," and it will guide you to some of the opportunities to become wiser — before you get too much older!

Is This Book For You?

If you or someone close to you face any of the changes listed below, then this book is sure to be of help.

- divorce or separation, the end of an important relation-ship
- new intimate relationship
- death of someone close, a family member, or a friend
- major illness or accident — your own or that of someone close to you
- move to a new residence
- marriage
- birth of a child
- children leaving home or coming back again
- breaking an addiction
- retirement, your own or your life-partner's
- change of career field
- job change, either upward, downward or sideways
- change in boss, company structure, merger or acquisition
- starting or completing school
- starting a new business
- major success — your own or that of someone close to you

Even if you are not going through any of these changes right now, we think the book will help you understand the trials everyone experiences from time to time.

Although transitions usually are seen as resulting from a major change, each of us tends to go through the seven stage cycle (described in Chapter Two) even with everyday ex-periences. Since these situations usually involve little novelty or surprise, one is less likely to be aware of anything out of the ordinary. When a big change occurs, however, the ups and downs can become quite intense.

What's The Book All About?

If you read through these pages and complete the exercises, we're sure you'll have a much better idea of how you can best help yourself weather the changes that are a big part of everyone's life experience. Also, as you find out that what you are going through is perfectly natural and very predictable, it probably will be less frightening for you to handle as you face the highs and the lows of "the change." Knowing that others have been through similar struggles can make it much easier to get through your own.

The seven-stage change sequence introduced in the next chapter (and covered in great detail throughout the book) gives you lots of information about what you can expect. Look at it as a map of the territory you will be crossing, with descriptions of what you are likely to find during your trip and some of the things you need to do to make sure you don't get lost. We'll even tell you how best to avoid getting stuck in "the swamps and the mires" that are often the most uncomfortable parts of the journey.

Like everyone else, of course, you'll make this journey in your own way. Some folks take the "highway," while others go via the "scenic route." You can actually turn the whole experience into quite a rewarding adventure if you are prepared. Our wish is that this book will give you many of the things you'll need to keep you safe as you move from the comfort of the known into the fear and excitement of the unknown.

We also want to help you discover some of your own special qualities so you can use them to help yourself through the "darker days" of a major transition. By working on the exercises throughout the book, you will feel a greater sense of self-esteem and recognize the many strengths you already have.

The book is divided into three parts: *Part One* describes "The Nature of Personal Transition," what it is and what can help you get through it. We'll talk about the common characteristics of any transition and give you a framework of the ideas we develop throughout the book. There's an overview of the normal, seven-stage sequence of adjustment that occurs when people make major changes, and a description of the many factors that can make a transition either more or less intense.

In *Part Two* we take you on a detailed journey through "The Seven Stages of Transition," complete with case examples and discussions of why each stage happens, what it's like, where you'll find support, and how to move on.

In *Part Three*, there is a lot of information on how to "Make the Most of It All." You'll find specific skills which will help you at times of transition, an exploration of how beliefs affect your experiences of change, ideas about how to keep a positive attitude in the midst of all the chaos, and ways to stay healthy during these often stressful times.

Toward the end of the book, we'll explore the value of a clear sense of life purpose, and how you can sometimes get out of balance and sick when you don't have one. The last chapter gives you ten steps that can help you not just *go* through life changes, but *grow* from them.

In the Appendix, there is a list of suggested readings many have found helpful. Some people who ordinarily don't read very much often gain enormous comfort from others' accounts of transition experiences, and become "book worms" during periods of personal change. These books provide a source of knowledge and comfort and describe some very exciting life experiences.

The menu ideas offer a guide for healthy eating during times of change (or at any other time). Our guidelines for a balanced diet prove that it really isn't too difficult.

How Best To Use The Book

There are many ways you can get the most out of this book and your own experiences of transition. One is to have a notebook or journal with you as you read through the pages, completing the exercises in each chapter as you go along.

Another way is to read the text and forget the exercises. It will take just an hour or two, and you will still get a good idea about the process of transition and what may happen to you as you go through a significant life change.

A third possibility: after you've figured out which of the seven stages you are in, turn to the chapter that covers that stage in detail and work through what you need to do in order to move on.

Whichever way you choose, we hope that you will find the stories, text, and exercises to be useful as you help yourself and others make the very most out of life's changes.

We hope you'll enjoy this book and that it will help you with your own life journey. By the time you've read it through, we think you'll feel that it was all worthwhile, and we're confident you'll face your world with a renewed sense of optimism.

2

WHAT IS TRANSITION ?

Transition is the "passage" of adjustment from one situation to another. It is triggered by a divorce, a house move, a change at work, the birth of a child — anything that requires an adjustment.

In our own lives, and in our work with thousands of others who have been going through changes, we've found that transitions seem to follow a predictable pattern. Most people we've met find that understanding this pattern helps them in at least two ways. First, it helps them see that, although their experience is unique in many ways, there is at least some predictability in the midst of all the chaos and confusion. Second, understanding the pattern of transition provides something to hold on to during the really tough times of the change process. That understanding can be a lifeline into the future when the past isn't there anymore, and the present is far from comfortable.

9

In this chapter, we'll provide a brief overview of this very natural and predictable pattern, and in Chapter Three we'll explore some common factors that affect how deeply you're likely to experience the seven stages of transition. As you read on, you'll make some interesting discoveries about your own past and the life changes you're experiencing. With a good understanding of the sequence that usually happens during major life changes, you'll find those in your life will be easier to handle.

The Process Of Transition

We've talked about the process of transition being both predictable and normal. Now let's go into it in more detail by describing the seven-stage sequence we've mentioned.

While there are some things you can do to speed up your passage through the uncomfortable parts of the process, we're sorry to report that we have not yet found any sure-fire ways to avoid those parts altogether. Actually, if you did manage to skip over the tough parts of the transition, you'd probably miss the best opportunities you have for increasing your potential in many different parts of your life.

An important thing to remember is that even though we present the stages of adjustment to change in a step by step fashion, your actual experience may not be linear. In any major transition, you may experience what we call "backing and forthing." From day to day, or even minute to minute, you may find yourself going from feeling strong and positive about the change to feeling overwhelmed and helpless. You may also find that you experience long periods of "feeling angry at the world" in the middle of one transition, and then hardly feel this at all during other periods.

One more thing: in order to bring the description of the seven stages to life as you read, we'd like you to take a few minutes now to answer some questions. Your answers will help you hook into the sequence more personally, and will give you a chance to compare your experience of a current or recent transition with our description of "the stages."

You may want to record your answers in a log or diary. There will be many times throughout this book when we'll suggest questions for you to think about — so you'll find it helpful to keep a notebook at hand as you read.

Transition Description Exercise
• Think of a significant change that has affected you personally. It will be more helpful if you choose a change that began fairly recently, and that you are still getting used to.
• Now, think of your transition as a series of steps, with a beginning, a middle period, and an end. The time line shown here is one way to look at these steps. Place a check mark (✓) somewhere along the line to show where you think you are at present.

BEGINNING   MIDDLE   END

——————————— TIME ———————————→

• Make some notes on what triggered this transition.
• Thinking only of the very *beginning* of this transition — the first few hours or days — how did you react or cope with it? What are some of the *earliest* feelings you remember?

• During the *middle* period, what are the things you remember the most, both good and bad, about coping with the changes? What feelings did you have?

• What are you doing at *present* about the transition and what feelings are you having about it right now?

• Thinking of the *future* (to the right of your checkmark), what are some of the challenges or experiences you think are yet to come before the adjustment to the change comes to an *end?* What feelings do you expect to have in the days ahead?

• Look over your answers to make sure your description is as complete as you can make it. We'll be coming back to this later, when we ask you to compare your transition experience with our description of the stages.

Transition And Your Mood

We have found it useful to fit the seven stages of transition to a mood curve as shown below. This helps describe how your mood might shift as you adjust to a major change. The curve may give you the idea that the experience is linear, so be sure to keep in mind that at one point you may "move" from left to right and at another, from right to left. It's also possible to get "stuck" somewhere along the curve for quite a long time.

STAGES OF TRANSITION

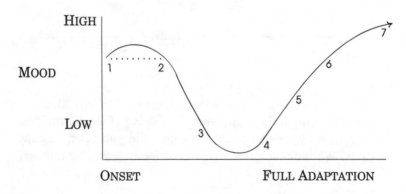

The dotted line near the left end of the curve means that in some cases people may not have an early "high" at the beginning of the transition. In most cases, if you are the one who decided to make the change, you may feel an early peak in mood. But when the change is "put" on you and is not something you want, you will probably feel quite a sudden drop in your energy or mood.

The Seven Stages Of Adjustment

The following brief descriptions will give you a flavor of what happens as people go through the sequence of adjustment to a change. In Chapters Four through Ten we will give you much more detail on each stage.

As you read over the next few pages, we'd like you to think about the personal transition experience you described earlier and relate it to the curve. If you'll take a moment to look at how it began, what's happened since, where you are now, and what you expect lies ahead, you'll find it much easier to relate our "stage" descriptions to your experience.

You'll also be able to see how far you've come in your current transition and get some ideas about what your next steps may be to move along the curve and complete the adjustment.

You may need to add a stage of your own to our model. Please adapt the curve so that it works for you. While many people find that these seven stages fit their experience, we want you to make this something useful in your life. So feel free to "play" with it.

Remember, whether the change is one you have chosen for yourself or one that has come as a surprise, you still are likely to experience all seven stages.

Stage 1: Losing Focus . As soon as you become aware that a change has begun, you are likely to experience a sort of numbness and feelings of unreality. It's rather like the experience of looking through a camera when the lens is out of focus; what used to look clear now seems fuzzy. You may even feel overwhelmed or shocked, and wander in a daze, forgetting where you were going!

> • *Patricia,* a participant in one of our workshops, remembered how for the the first few hours after being told she no longer had a job, she walked around in disbelief. She said her head felt as if it had been stuffed with cotton: "I couldn't believe it was true, and thought it was all in my imagination."*

Most people say that at the very beginning of a transition they had difficulty making plans or concentrating for very long. They were unable to think clearly or keep things in perspective.

One thing that can be learned as you pass through this stage is that any apparent stability in life is really only temporary; most of us are almost always experiencing one transition or another.

Stage 2: Minimizing The Impact. The most natural — or at least the most frequent — way people get through the early days is to pretend that it's "business as usual." They minimize the real impact of the change, at least to the eyes of the outside world.

It's a time of denial, and in some cases you may find you deny that *any* change has taken place at all, while putting lots of energy into appearing to be okay. Some people begin to drink more heavily, while others turn to over-indulging in their favorite foods.

> • *Bob, a close friend of ours, appeared to be very "high" for about a week after his partner died of cancer.*

---

*In the case examples throughout the book we have changed the names of the people whose experiences are included.

He was happy to tell everyone that her passing was beautiful and healing for all involved, and that he was doing great! For a while afterwards, he always seemed to have a drink in his hand. He said he was celebrating her freedom. It was over a month after her death before he began to admit that things weren't okay with him, and that he wasn't sure what he was going to do.

This stage provides you an opportunity to protect yourself, for a little while at least, from the full consequences of the change. It helps you to build the courage necessary for the journey that lies ahead — but staying too long at this stage can make the adjustment more difficult.

Stage 3: The Pit. Eventually, minimizing and denial don't work anymore, and reality begins to hit home. At this point, you will probably find yourself questioning everything from why all of "this" is happening to you to the very meaning of life. You may also encounter a growing sense of depression and powerlessness, experiencing little if any control over your present situation and how you are feeling.

Sudden bursts of anger and feelings of being stressed-out also are likely. So, too, are moments of intense sadness or grief. Even when the transition is one you have welcomed or chosen, the scope of the necessary adjustment is likely to create a period of self-doubt and questioning.

- *Lester had been involved in an accident at work that had taken the lives of two of his colleagues. Initially, he kept thinking how lucky he was to be alive and how he had gotten off easy. Then, he said, "it hit me like a ton of bricks." One minute he would be okay, and the next he'd be weeping uncontrollably. He even began to question why he had been the one to live, and wondered if he'd ever be "normal" again.*

At this stage, it is important to accept that it's okay to feel sad or angry, and that the harder you *try* to get over the distress, the longer it is likely to last. (You may even move back to Stage Two if you push too hard to get through this often painful stage.) The best advice we can give is to allow yourself all the time it takes to *fully* finish this stage of grieving before moving on.

Stage 4: Letting Go Of The Past. Up to this point, people tend to spend a lot of time thinking about the past. Once the grieving has run its course and you begin to come to terms with your loss, you'll probably feel ready to start up the other side, looking to the future. Although at first it may be difficult to let go, there probably will come a moment when you know you can do it, and from then on it will get easier. This stage is also a time of forgiveness.

> • *Mary had been separated for six months when she woke up one morning and felt as if the pain of being abandoned was beginning to fade. She said that she could at last see herself being okay, and all of a sudden she felt a new kind of confidence about starting a new life. She told us, "It was as if a little voice inside me was saying 'All right Mary, it's time to get on with your life!' She knew she had a long way to go, but she had begun to look forward.*

This turning around often feels like a breakthrough, and brings with it a new sense of optimism as you begin to put energy into creating your future. Often, however, there is something we call "the pendulum period," during which you may feel like you're on your way up the other side one minute, only to drop back into the pit the next. This is natural; it can take time to let go of the old situation, and you will need to be patient and gentle with yourself.

Stage 5: Testing The Limits. This is an exciting stage
—full of energy and enthusiasm. As you break free of the past
and step into the future with renewed confidence, you will
actively look for ways to test yourself in the new situation to
find out how far you can go.

You are establishing your "new self" by trying out new
behaviors and developing new skills. You could sometimes
find yourself feeling like a missionary, having "seen the light,"
and wishing to pass it on to others. Your zeal may even be too
much for others to take.

  • *Karen, the Human Resources Advisor at a hospital,*
  remembered that, about a month after getting promoted
  to her new job, she felt like she could solve every organiza-
  tional problem imaginable. She told us, with some em-
  barrassment, that she later learned she had offended a
  number of people with whom she worked during this time
  because she had wanted to change everything as soon as
  she took over. She also said she found herself going back
  into "the pit" for a little while after she realized she'd gone
  too far too soon.

The most common experience of this stage is a growing
sense of self-confidence that comes from being in charge of
your life, and feeling good about your new direction. It's also
a good time to have some friends around just in case you get
over-zealous and step beyond the limits. They can bring you
back — if you don't frighten them away.

***Stage 6: Searching For Meaning* .** During this stage,
you are likely to look back over the transition and try to figure
out the meaning of the change for your life as a whole. You
will feel a gradual shift in your energy, from being very active
and involved in Stage Five to spending more time alone,
reflecting on what you've been through, and trying to understand what it has all meant. As you sort through the ex-

perience, you'll begin to uncover all the "treasures" that you've found as you journeyed through the curve.

You may also decide to begin working with others who have just begun the kind of adjustment you've just been through. For example, if your transition was triggered by divorce you may want to help someone else through a divorce; if it was about losing someone close to you, you may want to help others through their grieving. It is at this stage when many people want to share the wisdom they've gained from their own experience.

> • *As the Soviet Union withdrew its troops from Afghanistan, a number of American Vietnam veterans went to Moscow to help their Soviet counterparts adjust to being home. When asked why, one American veteran reported, "When you've been through something as intense as we've been through and grown from it, there comes a time when you feel that you have to give something back."*

Stage 7: Integrating. After standing back and finding out what all of this has meant to you, you'll be able to put your discoveries and experiences into your everyday life. As these begin to sink in and become second nature, you'll find that you are looking at the world in new, more confident ways, without having to stop and think about it.

It's now safe to assume that, with the exception of the odd "flashback," the transition is as good as complete. You are sure to continue to learn new things from the whole experience that you've just been through, but most of your time and energy will now be focused on other things — and who knows, maybe your next major transition is waiting right around the corner.

We know from our own experiences that it can be very tempting to try to hurry through the transition process and skip the painful parts. But we've also found out that if you do avoid certain stages during one major change, they seem doubly intense the next time around.

The more you can just allow this process to run its natural course and not be tempted to push it along or pretend you're further along than you are, the more you're likely to find peace with yourself and feel a lot stronger. By being open to everything that comes along in each stage, you'll be able to make the most out of every experience, and feel yourself growing in knowledge and wisdom.

3

HOW MUCH WILL IT HURT?

People talk about their experiences of transition in many different ways. Some have described a "wave of change," while others talk of a whole string of surprising "chain reactions." Some say they felt they were riding on a roller coaster, clinging to the back of a tiger, traveling on a train, or lost in a tunnel, wondering if things would ever get back to normal.

There are some factors which seem to influence how deeply you'll experience a given transition and how much it will disrupt your life.

• The first of these factors is *novelty,* or how much the change takes you by surprise or puts you in an uncertain or unfamiliar situation. If the experience put you "in the dark" in some important way, that usually means you will be more acutely aware of the seven stages of the transition process. It often also means that you will spend more time "backing and forthing" among the stages.

We have been told by others, and found out for ourselves, that you can experience high levels of surprise quite "out of the blue" even in wanted, self-chosen changes. Often, what appears to be an "easy," wanted, transition, like moving to a new home, turns into a novel experience when you discover that you can't get the same goods or services that you relied on at your old location, or that the quality of relationships with your new neighbors is very different than "back home."

• The intensity of the seven stages also is influenced by how clearly you understand your own *expectations* of the outcome of the change. People with a clear vision of what they want at the end of the change usually experience less intensity and seem to move through the sequence more quickly.

If the transition is one you have chosen for yourself, it's not too difficult to develop some pretty clear expectations before getting started. On the other hand, if you are taken by surprise (high novelty), establishing a set of clear expectations will be much more difficult, but it will still need to be done as soon as you feel up to it.

We've learned that expectations don't always have to be absolutely "right," so long as you're willing to change them as you get new information. If you have no expectations, for example, about how a new relationship will develop for you, you may have a tougher time adjusting than if you have some early hopes that you're happy to change as things unfold. There are some people, on the other hand, who prefer to take each day as it comes and are happier just to go with the flow.

• Your *stage of life* at the time of a major transition can be key in determining both the amount of pain you will feel and the speed with which you move through the seven stages. As described by Gail Sheehy in *Passages* and Daniel Levinson in *Seasons Of A Man's Life,* some periods of our lives are more stable, while others are predictably more turbulent. "Mid-life crisis" is the most frequently cited example of an unstable and self-questioning period.

Major changes — such as marriage, divorce, career moves — made during a stable life stage will probably be less painful and require less energy to adjust to than if you make them during a more "uncertain" life period.

• The *number of other transitions* already under way also has quite an impact on intensity. If you are in the process of coming to terms with a divorce and one of your parents dies without warning, you will probably experience both transitions more deeply than if you only had to face one at a time.

This is also related to the "stage of life" you are in. A major transition can sometimes be the trigger that moves you into a turbulent life stage. The passages through a life stage and between life stages may also be thought of as transitions.

Also, taking on one change, such as a divorce, often triggers other major transitions, such as a residence move, changes in relationships with children, changes in social life, beginning a new intimate relationship, and even making a career change. It is not unusual for any one of us to be experiencing lots of transitions on top of each other, all of them taking an enormous amount of energy and pushing up the stress levels.

If you have the choice of how many changes you take on at once, we'd suggest that you tackle only one "big one" at a time. (This, we realize, may be easier said than done.)

• How well you handle your own and others' *emotions* is also important in determining how intensely you'll experience the transition. Some people are very much in touch with their feelings, while others prefer to "live in their heads." There are no rules in this area, but it seems that those people who are able to express their emotions find it easier to move through the difficult parts of the curve.

If you are going through more than one significant change at a time, you may experience a "spillover effect." That is, you may feel angry and frustrated over trivial things that have nothing to do with the change because your emotional "bucket" is full. Being able to release feelings in acceptable ways can help you move more quickly and less painfully through the transition curve.

• An obvious factor, although sometimes difficult, especially in Stage Two, is telling yourself the *truth* about what's really going on in the middle of a life change. Our western culture generally places a high value on being publicly "okay." In most places, you won't be encouraged to express your feelings of uncertainty, sadness, and anger. Rather, you'll most likely be rewarded for keeping a "stiff upper lip" or being "gutsy." How often have you felt lousy or upset about something, yet answered "fine" or "great" when someone asked you how you were? A lot of us do it a lot of the time.

One of the costs of fitting into our "be okay" world is that it becomes difficult to tell even *ourselves* the truth. Unfortunately, the more you deny to yourself the real impact of a change, the longer it is likely to take for you to come to terms with the new situation. Refusing to be clear with yourself can also make the transition process more painful and hold you back from moving through the stages.

Keep an eye out for any tendencies you may have to over-indulge in alcohol, cigarettes, caffeine, even chocolate. This can be an early warning that you are keeping something inside that needs to be expressed and it can be a way of trying to protect yourself from the truth.

• *Self-awareness* seems to have a major influence on the intensity and length of a transition. Each of us has peculiar quirks, temperaments and ways of doing things. The more aware you are of the many different parts of yourself, the better prepared you'll be to handle the stresses and strains that come with life's transitions. You'll also find more opportunities for personal growth and for increasing your self-confidence as you become wiser and more aware of the deeper purpose and meaning these changes have for you.

• The final factor we've identified, (although there probably are many others) has to do with setting *time boundaries*. The transition sequence is apparently, and unfortunately, very elastic. If there is a specified ending time, such as with a two- week vacation or a twelve-month work assignment, the pace of the transition is "pre-set," and you will probably travel the curve to fill the time available. It seems that when we set ourselves an endpoint, we unconsciously pace ourselves to complete the entire cycle in the time available.

Some friends of ours tested this when they had overseas assignments — one for six months and the other for two years. They each kept records of their cross-cultural adjustments. When they compared notes, they found they had completed the same sequence of stages — one moving four times faster than the other.

Unfortunately, setting time boundaries doesn't mean that you'll be able to skip through a major change in a matter of weeks just by setting yourself a deadline. The full transition process must run its course. But setting a realistic endpoint or at least some short-term goals that can always be changed can really help speed you along the curve. If the transition stays open-ended, the adjustment may take quite a long time to complete.

One powerful example of this was the return of veterans from Vietnam. Because of the open-ended nature of their return — and probably also because of the lack of clear expectations and support — their period of the readjustment was extended considerably. Not until several years after

returning home, did a large number of veterans hit bottom —
"the pit" (less than halfway along the transition curve). Only
then did they begin seeking professional counseling and setting up self-help support groups. At the beginning of the
1990's, disproportionate numbers were still jobless, homeless,
and/or in jail. More have committed suicide in the years
following their return home than the 60,000 who were killed
in action in Southeast Asia (Hearst, Newman and Hull, 1986).
Over half of all those who were exposed to combat in Vietnam
have experienced moderate to severe Post Traumatic Stress
Disorder (Kulka, et al., 1988).

Personal Notes On Patterns Of Adjustment
• Before moving to the next chapter, look over these
eight factors together with the change you described in Chapter Two and note the areas that need your special attention.

> *Novelty*
> *Expectations*
> *Life-stage*
> *Number Of Other Transitions*
> *Emotions*
> *Truth*
> *Self-awareness*
> *Time Boundaries*

What can you do to make sure that they don't "get to you"
too much during the transition?
• Remembering some of your past transitions, what really helped and what was not so hot?
• A lot of people find that important transitions bring
major life issues into focus. We each seem to have some very
basic questions we ask as we go through life. These are some
of them:

Question	Life Issue
Who Am I?	*Identity*
How Good Am I?	*Competence*
Where Do I Belong?	*Loyalty*
What's Next?	*Action*

Do some or all of these fit you, or do you have others?

It is probably obvious that whatever your questions, no single one is more or less important than any of the others. However, most of us will favor one over the others throughout our lives. Especially during times of transition, it is important that you know how the changes affect your search for the answers to these life questions. If you know which of these life issues fit you best, you will get the most from your transitions. Knowing that everyone has a different set also helps people to see that they don't have to experience life in the same way others do. *Vive la différence!*

• To finish this chapter, look over your notes and highlight those things:

a) you are doing well and want to continue

b) you want to stop doing or do less of

c) you want to begin doing more of

that will help to reduce the pain and intensity of the transition for you.

You may find that you need to spend more time with people who really understand you and care about you. You may decide that you need to get some more information or learn new skills to help with the change. Or you may find that you need to find some people who've already been through what you're now experiencing and will share ideas about what to expect.

As you begin the exploration of the seven stages of transition in Part Two, we urge you to go back to your notebook and have a quick look at the transition experience you wrote about in Chapter Two and also the lists from this Chapter of your various transition experiences to date. The more you can relate your own experiences to the points we are exploring, the more sense they will make.

CATHERINE'S STORY

Catherine had been married for almost eight years when Bill came home one day and told her that he wasn't happy with their relationship. At first, she thought it was just a passing phase and she soon forgot about it, but when he told her that things had not improved, and that he had met another woman, she said she was dumbfounded.

She tells what happened:

"I didn't know what to do. I was so surprised I couldn't think straight. It was only twenty degrees outside, but I just got up and went for a walk wearing only jeans and a T-shirt! I had to get out of the house to see if I could clear my mind. I must have been gone for over an hour but it never really felt that cold to me. I think I was numb with shock.

"By the time I got home I had talked myself into believing that nothing was really going to come of it all. I sat down to dinner and told him about my day and what I would be doing for the rest of the week. Bill was stunned at how laid back I was, but I continued as if everything were fine. I think I knew at some level that I was really hurting, but I sure as hell wasn't going to admit it to myself!

"For the next three months, he would stay out late and I could smell perfume on his clothes, but still I didn't say anything. I can't believe how I kept it all inside. I didn't even tell my closest friend. I guess I was treating it as a bad dream.

"One morning in early March, I woke up feeling sick and terribly confused. It was as if the dark cloud I'd been hiding from had suddenly caught up with me. I remember wanting to scream, 'Why, why, why? How could he do this to us?' When he got home late that night, I was waiting. I was so angry with all his games, and told him it was either her or me. He left the next day.

"I guess I went back into denial for a couple of days; I couldn't believe he wasn't going to come back. But this time I couldn't fool myself for long, and the dark cloud descended. For a while I tried to think it was all for the best, but then I began to sink lower and lower. I wondered whether to commit suicide because life was so unbearable. I had never felt so desperate. I looked terrible and didn't want to see anyone. Luckily, I had a wonderful woman friend who had been through a divorce. Although she had been the one to leave, Mary seemed to know just what I was going through.

"I had never thought of myself as an angry person, so it was a terrible shock when I started thinking terrible thoughts about destroying his new relationship. It was like being possessed by rage, and it terrified me because I didn't recognize myself. I remember driving around in the car, screaming and shouting and calling him names. Nobody could hear me, but it sure felt good to do it. My jaw ached by the end!

"For awhile, the anger came and went. I was going to make him really pay for the divorce one minute, and the next, I just wanted to run away and hide. It was so confusing. I never thought I would find anyone to love me again, and I didn't think I would ever trust another man. My work was suffering, and after losing ten pounds earlier on, I had now gained twenty-five. I'd stopped exercising and was living on coffee and danish.

"One evening, I sank so low that I couldn't see how I could ever feel alive again, and I went to bed hoping I wouldn't wake up. With only Mary to talk to and now convinced that I was going out of my mind, there didn't seem to be a reason to go on. Bill and I had decided not to have kids, so I didn't even have children as a comfort. I was so lonely! I started to cry and wound up sobbing uncontrollably for hours, wondering whether I'd ever stop; but I didn't care anymore. I cried myself to sleep.

"Something must have happened that night because when I got up the next day I felt different. It was as if I was lighter in some peculiar way. I could breathe deeply for the first time in months. By the time I finished breakfast, the feeling had gone and I was back at the bottom. For a moment it felt worse than ever; I thought this would never end. But later in the day, I had the same good feelings I'd had in the morning, and this time it lasted for a couple of hours before things became dark again.

"By the weekend, I began to feel better. I began to see that I could live without Bill. I didn't need a man! It was great, and I knew somewhere inside that the worst was over and I was going to make it! For the next few weeks I went back and forth, feeling really strong one minute, then feeling like a wet rag the next. In my strong hours, I would think about what I was going to do; maybe I could go on vacation, do all those things I had envied my unmarried friends for.

"Then the rest of the time, I'd just cry. I'd have to keep going to the bathroom at work so they wouldn't know what was happening. Soon there were more bright days than gray ones. It had been eight months since we'd separated, and I was beginning to feel quite good about myself. I packed up all Bill's clothes and sent them to him (I thought about burning them but changed my mind). I threw out all the letters he'd written to me over the years, and I splurged on some new clothes.

"In November, I took a much-needed vacation and had a great time with three of my women friends. I still found it hard to be with married people, and I turned down a wedding invitation because I knew I couldn't face it. For a while, I couldn't understand why anyone would want to get married and I swore I'd never do it again. In fact, I was so happy to be single again that I was convinced it was the only way to be. Anyone who wasn't must be crazy! I was a little wild for a while.

"After Christmas, I began thinking about having a relationship, but I wanted to play the field. It was great because I'd never done it as a teenager. I had a lot of fun and decided that I might get married again — one day.

"The divorce was final in April, and I thought I was going to fall right back into the depths again — and for a little while I did. Then I started to slow down a little and think about all that had happened in the past year. I was certainly different; I'd learned a lot about myself and felt much stronger and independent. I felt much wiser about life and more accepting of other people. I was no longer wrapped up in my security blanket, but was awake and somehow more interested in life. I had even begun doing some community work, something I had never dreamt of before the divorce. I had some of the darkest moments of my life, and hope I will never have to go that low again.

"Now, after two years, I don't think about it much anymore. I have some emotional scars, but the incredible confusion and craziness is gone. I have some flashbacks about the happier days with Bill, and I'm looking forward to maybe marrying again and having or adopting a child. I don't think I'd change anything now, but if I had one bit of advice for someone going through something like this, I'd tell them to talk to more people. There are lots out there ready to help and I really didn't have to do it all by myself."

PART TWO

THE SEVEN STAGES OF TRANSITION

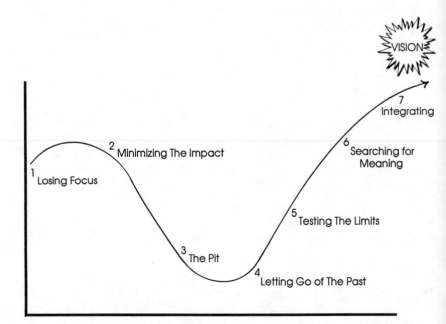

4

STAGE ONE:
LOSING FOCUS

Who rocked the boat and took a chance
to change this path I'm on?
Was it you or me or circumstance?
I'm confused, the familiar is gone...

Author William Bridges, in his own excellent book on transitions, points out that the beginning of a transition is also an ending of something else — a relationship, a job, a stage of life. Not only do you have to take the new situation in, but you also have to let go of some aspect of the past situation.

At the beginning of a major change you're likely to feel flooded with new information, as well as sense the loss of something familiar. This can cause your poor old brain to become fuzzy and overloaded. As a result, you are likely to feel confused about where the boundaries are and what your priorities need to be.

What It's Like

Our workshop participants often describe this first stage as being "spaced out." There usually is a sense of feeling numb or in a daze, and it is difficult to stay focused for any length of time. Everything seems fuzzy.

> • *Jean, whose husband had left her, said that at first her mind was like a butterfly, flitting from thought to thought, and never staying put for more than a few seconds. She said she was quite confused and couldn't plan very well — she kept forgetting what it was she was doing. She said, "There were times when I would find myself in a store or in a meeting and have no idea why I was there, and I'm normally such an organized person!"*

In cases where the change is very high in novelty — surprise and unfamiliarity — you may find yourself feeling completely overwhelmed and frozen by feelings of panic or even terror. When this happens, people talk about spending a few days drifting in an unreal world, feeling as if all their energy has been drained. Some even say they felt as if they'd been stunned and wondered if people subjected to "shock therapy" feel this way.

You may also have feelings of incredible excitement with this first stage of the transition process, especially if the change is one you really wanted.

> • *A Dutch colleague told us of how he became almost "out of control" with excitement when his partner had told him she was pregnant. He found it difficult to remain sitting for more than a moment and was unable to concentrate for several days. "I wanted to tell the whole world about it!" he said.*

Another thing you're likely to find, if your change has a lot of novelty, is that you are acting completely out of character for a period of time. People who are normally extraverted often become quiet and withdrawn, while those who are normally introverted may suddenly become very talkative. Those who are usually practical and down to earth may start to dream and fantasize, while those who usually like to muse about the future become very pragmatic and detail-focused. People who take pride in their logic may become highly emotional, and those who make their decisions based on their feelings suddenly become very cool and thoughtful. Decisive people become reluctant to make a decision, while those who generally keep things open ended suddenly find a sense of urgency to complete things.

Where You'll Find Support

One of the most supportive things you can do at this early stage is to spend time with close friends willing to "just hold on and listen to you jabber nonsensically." Many report that they found a lot of comfort in surrounding themselves with familiar "things" to reassure them that not *everything* was changing.

For many people — and you'll know if you're one of them — the onset of a crisis "causes" them to give up their good habits and "indulge" in activities that can damage their long-term health. It is not unusual in this stage for smokers to smoke more, for ex-smokers to start again, or for drinkers to drink more. People who take regular exercise often quit and those who normally have a balanced diet eat more junk food if they bother to eat at all. Many in our "I have to be okay" society withdraw from friends who could provide the support they need, because they feel uncomfortable showing vulnerability.

How To Move On

Fortunately, this "fuzzy" first stage usually doesn't last too long. Even if you do nothing to help bring it to an end, you're likely to find yourself passing to the next stage quickly.

For some, Losing Focus only lasts for a couple of hours. For others, it may be a few days. We've rarely heard of it lasting any longer.

There are, nevertheless, a few things which people have found helpful. All the ideas have to do with very short-term "earthy" activities. It seems that one of the best ways to manage this first stage of transition and encourage movement to the next one is to make a very specific "to do" list — and follow it. For example, "By noon I'll get the laundry done;" "I'll have the car washed at 3:00;" "I'm going to weed the garden as soon as I finish this cup of coffee." Remember that this is the stage where everything is a little "fuzzy" and it's very easy to forget things.

> • *One young woman told us that only hours after she heard her mother had died she went to the supermarket to buy enough food for the family for the week they would be away for the funeral! As she was on her way home, she remembered that she'd left her two year old daughter sitting in a shopping cart at the supermarket. Writing a "to do" list won't prevent this from happening but it will help keep you focused — if at the time you can find a piece of paper and a pen.*

We don't recommend lengthy meditation during Stage One of transition, as you are already likely to be more out of focus than you'd like to be. If you do meditate regularly, you may find that a few days off is helpful, otherwise you may feel very frustrated with yourself as all the mixed up thoughts call out for your attention. Try a more focused activity, such as thinking about what today would be like if it were ideal, or planning what you need to do today.

It seems to us that the most important thing you can learn from this period of Losing Focus is to recognize that long-term stability is one of life's illusions. Even if you think there is less going on in your life today than there was yesterday, things are always in a state of flux. Change clearly has become a contemporary way of life, but sometimes we don't recognize it until we find ourselves faced with a situation that sends us on the transition journey through the stages of the curve.

One activity that many have found helpful is the use of affirmations. We talk about this further in Chapter Fifteen as a way of "reprogramming your mind" to think more positively. In each of the seven stages there are some common areas of confusion or struggle that can cause you to feel down or out of control. To help you through these periods, we have prepared some suggested affirmations you can repeat to yourself whenever you feel you're about to go under. You may also wish to create some affirmations of your own.

Common Areas Of Confusion	Suggested Affirmations
Who am I and what do I want?	*I am alive and growing.*
Can I handle this?	*I am able to face any challenge.*
What should I do next?	*I know what I need to do.*
Am I doing the right thing?	*I trust myself to do what is right.*

Key Growth Opportunity: Accepting that stability is always temporary!

Personal Notes On Stage One
- As you think about the first moments of a current transition, perhaps the same one you described in Chapter Two, — and the beginning of others you've been through —

write down what your immediate reactions and feelings were.

- Is there a consistent or predictable pattern in your reactions? If so, what is it?
- How well did you look after your health during this stage?
- What do you need to keep doing, or do more of, or do less of?
- What seem to be your most typical areas of confusion and which affirmations would be particularly helpful?

As you look over your answers, identify something you could do today that would help you feel more grounded.

Are You Ready for Stage Two?

You'll know you're on your way to Stage Two when you find yourself saying that it was "just a flash in the pan," and you feel an urgent need to get things back to normal. You'll be doing your utmost to maintain an "I'm okay" attitude and will want to appear "on top of it all" to the outside world.

5

STAGE TWO:
MINIMIZING THE IMPACT

Please don't ask me how I am;
I'm hiding from my pain.
And no one knows (least of all me)
when I'll find peace again.

You can only operate for so long with your mental and emotional circuits on overload. A few days after the start of a major change, you'll probably find yourself moving into "remote control" to protect yourself from further input from the outside world. It is natural to behave as if everything is perfectly normal, giving yourself and others the illusion of having everything under control.

You even may hear yourself saying things like "I'm fine," or "This change isn't going to make much difference to my life," or "I've been getting myself ready for this for some time." And then after a couple of weeks of feeling a little down, thinking to yourself, "I'm over 'it' now."

People tend to minimize the true impact of a change, and sometimes deny it altogether, because there's a need to get ready on so many different levels to adjust to the consequences. If we did it all at once we'd probably go crazy. With any life change, there is a lot that's new and a lot that must be let go. It takes time to sort through some of the early thoughts and emotions that accompany a major transition. So, while all this is going on under the surface, you may say to yourself and others that everything is fine, and you mean it at the time.

This second stage is an essential part of the transition process because it helps to heal and protect us in the short term. However when people get stuck in the "Dance of Denial" and won't accept the reality of the change, they often become dependent on alcohol or drugs, or bury themselves in their work.

What It's Like
Many who have chosen to make changes report a sense of freedom and sometimes experience a real "high" during the early part of Stage Two — a sudden "burst of energy" that's been waiting to be released. It's the sense of euphoria that often follows the birth of a child, graduation, getting married, finding a new job, or receiving a promotion.

> • *On their wedding day, some friends of ours were both very excited. They had told us and others that being married really wasn't going to be a big change because, after all, they'd been living together for nearly two years. They had to eat those words.*

When the change is an unwelcome surprise, the euphoria is sometimes, though not always, missing. There is, nevertheless, an outward show that "everything's okay."

Many participants in our workshops have told us that this stage feels like a continuation of the unreality of Stage One and that they feel as if they're drifting in a "sea of timelessness." Others remember a sense of being disoriented and walking around saying "everything's fine" over and over again, knowing that underneath that things were really not so hot.

> • *Sam had been working for the same company for twenty-five years and believed that as long as he did a good job he would stay there until retirement. He was absolutely dumbfounded when he was told that in three months, owing to a major cutback in personnel, there would no longer be a role for him.*
>
> *Sam did not tell his family what happened for several weeks, and began going to work earlier than usual and staying later. He wouldn't talk about it with his co-workers and carried on as if everything were the same as it had always been.*

Another example is given by C. Murray Parkes in his book on bereavement (see References). Parkes investigated how widows in London reacted to the deaths of their husbands and found that many women would not dispose of their husbands' clothes for several months after their deaths. They found it difficult to accept that "he would not be coming home."

During this period in a significant transition, nearly everyone moves into feeling a little more defensive than usual and denies that anything's different. Friends and family, however, are often aware that there is something "wrong" and begin to pick up the signals of pain and confusion. In some cases, people have said that they've actually stopped seeing friends, or started staying out longer, to keep the illusion that they were doing fine.

But, inside, there's usually a growing sense that there has been a loss or an ending, as well as the beginning of something new, and that some important adjustments will need to be made. As in Stage One, there may be some subtle changes in personality.

A number of people have told us that rather than acting out of character they tended to exaggerate their normal ways of behaving — extraverts became more outgoing, and introverts spent more time focused deep inside; people who like details became nit-picky, while those who prefer to focus on the "big picture" drifted into day dreaming and gave people the impression that they'd gone a little "wacky." Those people who work a lot with logic experienced "analysis paralysis," and those who usually make decisions depending on how they "feel about something" found themselves up to their eyes in all sorts of conflicting emotions and values. Those who are generally quick at making decisions began reaching hasty conclusions about everything, while the easy going "go with the flow" folks found it difficult to get *anything* done.

All this happens because we need to convince ourselves that everything is okay, while on another level, our minds and emotions are trying to come to grips with the consequences of a great deal of disruption. Eventually, we'll have to come to terms with what has been gained and what has been lost, which is the focus of the next stage on the curve. We can't run away forever, although some people find ways to extend Minimizing for a very long time and become dependent on alcohol, drugs, or other forms of addiction.

Where You'll Find Support

Getting support at this stage of the transition is a bit tricky because the message you're sending (and believe to be true) is that you are doing just fine and really don't need anyone's help at all. Therefore, most of your support will have to come from inside yourself as you try to make sense of everything.

Some of the ideas we talked about in the last chapter will also be useful here. Short-term simple activities, keeping "busy" and taking just one step at a time will be most helpful during Stage Two. You may also find it helpful to get others to accept that you *really are okay for now,* and to ensure that they'll be there for you when you need them — which might be a little sooner than you think.

Once more, it is not unusual for people to forget to look after themselves at this time. They often seek to escape from growing confusion and loss of control by eating and drinking too much. If you do nothing else, we really encourage you to watch closely what you eat and drink, and to engage in some kind of daily exercise and relaxation practices. (See Chapter Sixteen for some ideas.)

How To Move On

To move through this stage effectively, do your best to tell yourself the truth about what is *really* going on. If you can accept that you may be putting a lot of your energy into minimizing the impact of the change and accept also that it's perfectly okay to do so for a while, then you are likely to move on without much difficulty.

We have met people who spend a long time in this stage, denying that anything has changed or that they're feeling any sense of loss or pain. Others will undertake a new transition each time the real impact of the present one begins to hit home. We often hear of people ending relationships as soon as things get a little uncomfortable — believing that if it were "right" they would always feel good together. These people find themselves drifting from one relationship to another, never moving beyond Stage Two of the transition process.

Telling the truth and finding others who will help you face up to what is happening are among the best ways to move you forward at this stage.

There is another tactic that many have found useful. Once you begin to acknowledge that you've been playing it safe, just pick up a pen and write down whatever comes to mind. Don't try to have it make sense or worry about such things as spelling. Just let it write itself. This is variously known as "free associating," or "automatic writing," and it can help you let go of the rational control that may stop you from saying what you *really think and feel.* You'll probably find it very liberating and be pleasantly surprised at how creative you are when you stop censoring yourself. After you've done this for a few days, review what you've written, searching for themes or patterns that can help you understand what's going on.

Keeping a journal which tracks your feelings and thoughts will help you stay in touch with what's going on in your inner world, especially when you appear to be doing great on the outside. Our participants say they found it fascinating to look back at the notes they made to themselves, because everything that was *really* going on was written down, while on another level they went on about their lives as if none of it were happening.

One of the most useful assets to develop during this stage is courage — being unafraid to take action even in the face of fear or personal risk. It is in Stage Two that you will need to take an honest look at what's going on and then act in ways that will move you forward, even though it may seem hazardous at the time. Summon your courage, and take the necessary steps.

Typical Areas Of Confusion

Suggested Affirmations

Why do I have these feelings? I'm sure I'd be better off without them.

My feelings are very valuable!

What if I lose control?

I am learning and growing!

What would others think if they knew what was really going on inside my head?

I am true to myself!

Key Growth Opportunity: Building courage. Taking risks.

Personal Notes On Stage Two
- Are you able to see how you typically react in this stage? What are some of the things that you do to minimize the impact of a change?
- As you think back over other transitions in your life, what have you done that worked well for you during this stage?
- Are there any changes you would make next time?
- Think of someone close to you, whom you feel you can really talk to about what's going on — someone who will listen to whatever you have to say without judging you or trying to change you — and give him or her a call.

Are You Ready for Stage Three?
It will be easy for you to tell that you're moving into Stage Three: you'll begin to feel a growing sense of unrest, emotional discomfort and perhaps a hollow sense of loss. It's becoming more and more difficult to pretend to yourself and to others that everything is quite normal.

6

STAGE THREE: THE PIT

Who am I? I need to know. Is all of life a game?
Where is my strength and confidence,
my faithful inner flame?
How much longer will I doubt this power inside of me?
Before I trust the quiet voice
that gently sets me free?

Of all the stages, this one is usually described as being the most difficult to handle and the most painful. This is true whether the change was one you chose for yourself or one that was imposed by other people or by circumstances. It is only now that you are likely to face up to the fact that your life is going to be different and that you're leaving some important people or things behind you.

This stage of the transition journey is a time when you may begin to feel angry, sad, withdrawn or afraid as you recognize what you are losing. It is often here in Stage Three that you accept at last that things aren't the way they used to be — familiar faces and places are gone.

One way of looking at this period is as a time of healing any wounds left by the change, and as a clearing out of attitudes and behaviors which will no longer support you, so that there is room to take on what lies ahead. Expressing your feelings of sadness and anger can free up the energy you will need for the new situation or relationship. Keeping these feelings inside will take more and more energy and can hold you back from your next steps.

Being truthful with yourself about what you're *really* feeling will help you to shorten this stage. Trying to avoid this part of the process doesn't seem to work. Many of our participants have asked if there's any way of skipping Stage Three. We haven't found one yet, and we think that if you did skip it you'd probably miss out on some of the most rewarding parts of the whole transition experience.

Part of the reason this stage is so difficult is that most of us were not taught to grieve. We're supposed to carry on regardless. Children are told over and over to stop crying, and are often punished for getting angry. As a result you are likely to believe that feelings of sadness and anger are not okay, and if you do have them you should keep them to yourself.

Today, there is more acceptance and encouragement for people to express their emotions, and there even are suggestions that holding back anger and sadness can actually be harmful to health. This stage is a real opportunity to express any pain you may be feeling and to "make space" for the growth and development which is ahead for you.

What It's Like

There's no place to hide any more. Some of the feelings you denied in the previous stage are likely to catch up with you now. People find that even though they were not purposely hiding their feelings about the change, they did have a sense of the inevitability of this uncomfortable phase. Of course, how deeply you go down into "the pit" will depend on the factors we mentioned in Chapter Three. For some, it is a short period of depression, for others one of the toughest struggles of their lives. It's a time for coming face to face with some of your worst fears about yourself and about life. (We talk about fear in much greater depth in Chapter Eleven.)

However well prepared you might have thought you were, you'll probably be surprised at how low and how lonely you feel at times during Stage Three. You may feel as if something is sapping away your energy. For some, it is so dark that they find it hard to believe they will ever be happy again.

> • *Susan's husband had been killed in a plane crash and she had spent weeks drifting around feeling numb. Then she told of waking up one morning with a terrible feeling of rage; she began screaming at her husband for abandoning her "when we were just getting everything together." How dare he! Then she said she started to cry and was scared that she would never stop. At one point, she didn't think she wanted to go on with her life.*
>
> *For the next several months, Susan said, she would suddenly lash out at someone for no reason, or just burst into tears. She told us "it was as if a part of me had to die before I could begin living again."*

The depth of your depression during this stage may vary from a general lethargy or apathy about life to considering suicide. The anger that you focused at first on other people or "the system" begins to shift, and you may find yourself beginning a process of deep self-questioning. Depending on your personality, and the type of change you are undergoing, your questions are likely to fit into one or more of the following areas: Who am I? Am I any good — do I have anything to offer? Is there anything worth doing? Where do I belong — does anyone really care?

At such times, you may tend to hide away to lick your wounds in private. You may also find some of your thoughts and feelings — perhaps hatred and rage — to be quite terrifying; you're scared of what might happen if you really let it all out. Coming to terms with the "dark side" is a normal part of the transition experience. We encourage you to talk with a trusted friend, counselor or therapist about whatever feelings you experience. If you find it too difficult to talk about what's going on, then write it all out in a journal. It is vital that you clear all this "stuff" away; otherwise, it just seems to go round and round in circles, and so will you.

> • *Joe had married when he was twenty and had done everything he should to look after his wife and "provide" for her during the ten years they were together. One day, he came back from work to find a note telling him that she had found someone else who "understood" her and that their marriage was over. He was shattered; he tried to get her to come back, but she wouldn't. He began drinking heavily and wouldn't talk to anyone for quite a while. When he realized he couldn't run away from "it" anymore, he sank into what he described as a "black hole" and fought for his sanity. "It was so dense and dark, I never thought I would be normal again."*
>
> *Joe questioned everything. He no longer knew what to believe and realized that a lot of things he thought were true no longer had meaning for him. His whole view of the world turned upside down. He wrote pages of notes about everything he was feeling. Some of it was in the form of poetry. He now looks back at this time as being both the most terrifying and the most amazing time of his life.*

Many people experience a sense of being broken or bruised and feeling very vulnerable. Feelings of self-hatred and self-doubt are common companions. You may come to believe that you are unlovable or incompetent, and that your self-confidence has gone forever. You may also begin wondering about

the purpose of life and the nature — or the existence — of
God.

   • *When we first met Carol, she was struggling with
herself and her relationship with her mate. They had been
together two years when they found that he had multiple
sclerosis. As sometimes happens, she had felt that she
should be the tough one and keep a brave face. She told
people that everything was okay, and "it" really wasn't
going to make too much difference to their relationship.*

   *Her partner was being given plenty of support by
everybody, and he was beginning to come to terms with
what his disability would mean, while Carol continued
coping. It was six months later that the bubble burst, and
reality hit home. First of all, she was angry with him for
spoiling their relationship. Then she said she got angry
with the world and began to wonder whether there really
was a God.*

   *At work, she couldn't concentrate and her perfor-
mance began to suffer. She lost all interest in keeping
herself fit and healthy. It wasn't until she found that it
was okay for her to have these feelings — and that people
would not see her as selfish — that she began to put things
into perspective.*

   Whether the change is chosen or not, the questions during
Stage Three are many. People who get divorced question
whether they will ever trust enough to love again; those who
have chosen to marry or have a child question whether it was
what they really wanted. This is a very lonely time for many
people and they often have a sense that no one else could
possibly help or understand them.

   • *It was the second marriage for both Peter and Jane;
he had been divorced for two years and she had been on
her own for nearly six years. After a year of living*

together, they decided to get married. They were very much in love and really enjoyed each other's companionship.

Four months after the ceremony they felt themselves drifting apart — the connection they had felt so strongly seemed to disappear — and they both began to question their choice of partners. At first they just avoided each other, but then they began to fight. Jane got very depressed and kept remembering how free she had been when she was single; Peter kept remembering how much easier it had been with his first wife. It was another two months before they felt the deep and loving connection come back into their relationship and could stop focusing on what they'd each had to give up to be together.

Even with positive life choices, one must go through a very natural period of "grieving" for the old situation before the new can be let in fully.

Some people, to escape the pain and the questioning, find themselves returning to Stage Two. If you try this, you'll soon discover that you can't go back; the formerly safe and familiar place is no longer where you belong. You've had the courage to come this far and you can find more courage to see you through, no matter how dark it gets.

* *Keith was 43 years old and had been looking forward to his next promotion for two years. When it finally came, he was thrilled. But he said the good feelings didn't last long before he fell into the depths of despair and began getting very impatient with his wife and his children. He couldn't understand what was happening. At first he wanted to go back to his old job, but he knew that wouldn't solve the problem, so he decided to face up to all the fears and doubts.*

When we asked him what else could be adding to his bad feelings, he told us that his father had died only one year earlier, and that his new job would mean moving to another part of the country, leaving his friends and his mother behind. With the help of others in the workshop, Keith began to see that it was not just the promotion that was making him feel depressed, but that his age and other changes going on in his life were all adding to his loss of confidence and the changes in his behavior.

Once you are well into freeing yourself from some of these more uncomfortable feelings and beginning to understand why all of this is happening, you will discover a growing sense of self-esteem. Some people talk of amazing spiritual experiences, becoming aware of inner and outer "guides," and generally getting in touch with a deeper part of themselves. Others talk of feeling much more at peace with themselves. Whatever your experience, you are likely to begin feeling more powerful, more self-aware and more understanding of others.

Where You'll Find Support

At this point of the transition, you'll probably need some safe places to express your anger and hurt. Find people who love you enough to listen to what you have to say without judging you. Spend time with friends who will let you be yourself, whatever that might look like. If you're helping someone through this stage of the curve, the single greatest gift you can give is to listen with an open heart and an open mind, with no wish to "change" that person in any way.

If someone is telling you that you "shouldn't" feel that way, or that you "should" be over it by now, you need to find someone else, because the person you're talking with now is not hearing *you*. "Don't let anyone *should* on you, and never *should* on yourself!" Sometimes you may hear yourself say such things as, "I should remember how lucky I am," or "I should be grateful," especially if the change is one you have chosen. Stop yourself and say, "No more shoulds."

In the drawing below you can see that the "should" line suggests that you "should" move directly from Stage One to Stage Seven and some people will want you to do just that. You may even try to do it yourself in order to jump over "the pit." Although it would be nice if this were possible, you will find that if you try to avoid the natural transition process, you'll actually stay in Stage Two and lose out on opportunities for growing.

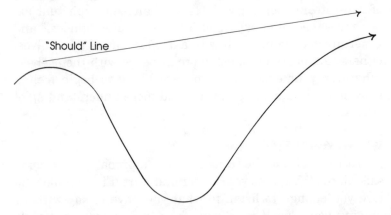

"Should" Line

You may also find yourself accepting full responsibility for what happened and not allowing yourself to feel the disappointment and hurt that comes when others let you down. Our experience is that people who don't express these feelings find that they "leak out," sometimes in the wrong place at the wrong time. Giving yourself permission to express fully and safely what is going on for you, even if it makes you uncomfortable, is likely to speed you through this stage.

When you do develop the courage to tell it as it really is, you'll find others who'll admit that they have had similar thoughts and feelings. Fears of being weird, odd, or even out of your mind, fade away as soon as you recognize that all of this craziness is a natural part of being human.

During Stage Three, people frequently tend to give up all their good habits.

If you normally avoid fatty foods you may find yourself eating more of them, ice cream and chocolate may become good "friends" at a time like this. If you smoke, you'll probably smoke more; if you exercise regularly, you'll probably let it slip; and if you have a tendency to use alcohol and drugs, you may begin taking these more frequently as a way of escaping the pain. If you do have a weakness for any of these substances, it is important that you keep an eye on how much you are using and seek help if you conclude that you are relying on them as crutches. Maintaining your physical health will affect how you feel about yourself as well as your outlook on life. Good health can make this stage much easier to get through.

Not too long ago, people who asked for support from therapists and self-help organizations like Alcoholics Anonymous or Weight Watchers were sometimes frowned on or thought of as being weak. Not anymore. Today, there are employee assistance programs in most larger organizations where people can receive counseling on personal matters as well as work or career issues. There is ample evidence to suggest that our society is becoming more aware of the impact change has on people: the availability of stress management programs, wellness activities, and community counseling services. You don't have go it alone anymore. If you reach out, someone will be there for you.

You may find therapy or counseling enormously valuable during Stage Three, as you work through some of these thoughts and feelings. Professional support can help you rebuild and strengthen your trust and confidence.

Sometimes, spending time outdoors with nature can help to put things into perspective. Being in the woods can have a very healing effect. Doing mundane activities like washing

dishes or sewing on buttons or cleaning the car can also help
you to stay grounded.

How To Move On

Stage Three can last from a few weeks to several months.
Avoid comparing your experience with others, or you'll
probably get into "shoulding." No two people's experiences are
exactly the same, although people with similar personalities
may have similar stories to tell.

It's *now* that you must start putting lots of energy into
looking toward the future. You don't have to take any big
steps, but it helps to give yourself some small successes so
that you can begin to move forward. People who get stuck here
are those who, years afterward, keep talking about the past
— "the good old days" — and won't think of the future. Their
attachment to "the way it was" is so great that they are unable
to see any other way of living. Unfortunately, we can't do
anyone else's work for them and people have to be ready to
move on. Skilled professionals are the best source of help for
those people who get stuck in Stage Three.

Taking a vacation after this often stormy time can help
the healing. So, too, can stepping out into new arenas and
taking small risks that are guaranteed to succeed. If you are
in the process of a divorce or have lost your spouse, this is the
time you might go to your first dinner party as a single person,
maybe with some very close friends so that if you feel a little
wobbly there is someone there to support you. If you've moved
to a new neighborhood you could invite a couple of your new
friends for dinner, or you could become involved in the local
community. Do some little things to begin building your new
world.

It may help you turn the corner if you close your eyes and
think of a time two years from now. Pretend that you have
been given a magic wand and can create an ideal day for
yourself. You can make it any way you want.

Take a moment and think about where you are on this ideal day and what you're doing. How are you feeling now that the transition is over and you're fully at home in the new situation? Are you with anyone, or are you on your own? Get a picture of yourself and your relationship to everything around you. Stay with the magic of your experience for a few moments, and then write down what you saw, felt and heard as if it were true right now. For example, "I am walking on a beach in bright sunshine. It's early morning and no one else is around. I feel bright and positive and have lost all the weight I gained during the transition. I'm at last enjoying living on my own, and..."

When you have written it out, read it through a couple of times and add anything else you would like to have on this ideal day.

Common Areas Of Confusion	Suggested Affirmations
Am I a good person?	*I am who I am and people love me.*
Will I ever get control of this?	*I am learning to trust mself.*
I am so afraid.	*People will help me.*
Why am I so emotional?	*I am growing.*
Will I ever trust anyone again?	*I am learning to love myself.*

Key Growth Opportunity: To get in touch with a deeper part of yourself and find more compassion and love for yourself and others.

Personal Notes On Stage Three
• What are your usual ways of dealing with your feelings at times like this?
• Write down anything else you could do to make it easier on yourself.
• What do you need to do more of — and less of — to stay healthy right now?
• Decide on at least one thing you'll do today to take care of yourself. Maybe just going for a short walk will help. List the ten things you enjoy most about being you (e..g. my sense of humor).
• List twenty things you really like doing (e.g. walking in the rain).

Think about the last time you did each of these things, and see if you can plan something fun for yourself this coming weekend. You deserve it. Whenever you're feeling down or lost, remember the things you enjoy about yourself and you enjoy doing; they're always there for you.

Are You Ready For Stage Four?
Can you see a light at the end of the tunnel? If your answer is yes, you're probably ready to move on. You may still be feeling a little bit down but you've confronted your fears and expressed feelings of anger and sadness. Your questions of self-doubt and concerns about losing control are being replaced by a sense of optimism and a "can do" attitude. You've accepted that you can't go back, and you have the strength to go forward.

7

STAGE FOUR:
LETTING GO OF THE PAST

Sometimes when the sun shines bright
a shadow falls that blocks the light,
and sadness fills the darkened spaces
while I heal those lonely places.

At some point you will stop wanting to look back to the past and begin putting your focus on creating a new future. The grieving is over and you know that the anger and questioning are no longer useful. You're now ready to stop walking backward into the future. It's time to turn around and face the direction you are going.

It often takes a lot of courage to move into Stage Four. There is comfort in holding on to the past, whatever it feels like, because at least it's familiar. As soon as you make the choice to let go, you accept the challenge of stepping into the unknown. For many, this is a major breakthrough.

The energy you free up will now be available for a different purpose, and you'll begin looking for the opportunities and better times that lie ahead. If you don't let go and make this shift in focus, there will be little energy to build the new situation. It takes an enormous amount of effort to continue to hold on once the time has come to move ahead.

If you take a look at the curve you'll see that Stage Three takes you right to the bottom. Once you are there you have three choices: to keep trying to go back the way you came, to stay in "the pit," or to let go and begin moving up the other side.

One way to look at this is to imagine that the part of the curve from Stage Two to Stage Four is covered in oil so even if you do manage to climb up some of the way you'll probably slip right back down again. Staying in "the pit" once your work there is done really has no purpose unless you want more of the same. The track from Stage Four to Stage Seven may be unfamiliar and a little steep but there are steps carved into the slope and you have all the skills and strength you need to make the climb once you decide you are ready to go. (There's a "transition skills questionnaire" in Chapter Thirteen which may be useful at this point.)

What It's Like

For most people this stage is the first time the sun shines after the storm. There is a sense of growing excitement despite a continued feeling of fragility as one makes the decision to face the future.

> • *Anne was forty-five when her last child went away to college. She had been working part-time for ten years, but had always seen it as something she could take or leave; her main role was as a mother.*
> *The first Christmas after the nest became empty, she was very depressed, questioning why she should carry on*

— nobody needed her anymore. The following March, she said, she awoke one morning and knew there was something more for her. Anne felt as if a heavy load had been lifted and she started to believe in herself again. She began making a new career for herself in the outside world and is now director of her own company.

Another thing that frequently happens at this time is an increase in "backing and forthing" between the stages — so much so that we call it "the pendulum period." You may feel great one day and then wake up the next asking some of the same old questions that take you back into Stage Three.

The first time this happens can be quite frightening. You thought you were "over it" by now. Don't worry. This is a perfectly natural part of the process. Remember that the new situation is still very fragile and the old one may still have a lot of power. This, coupled with our human tendency to resist change, means that often we have to work really hard to pull ourselves around this corner.

* *Mary's divorce had been very painful, but with the help of some friends she was able to get herself back together. There were many times when she wondered if she would make it, especially after a period of hallucinations which she told no one about.*

One evening she was lying on the couch alone in her apartment. "It was dark and I felt so full of fear that I knew death would be easier than this," she recalled. "I lay there for a while hoping for some answers, and then I heard a little voice inside myself tell me I was going to be all right, and I knew I would make it." She began pacing, telling herself over and over that she was going to be okay. That was the first night she went to bed feeling optimistic.

When she awoke the next morning it was a different story. She was back in the "dark" again and began to doubt herself. Later in the day, she felt the same sense of hope about the future, and this time it lasted longer before she went back to the questioning. This time, she wasn't as frightened because she knew that even if she went "under" she would come up again.

During the "letting go" stage you may also make a quick return to Stage Two or shoot ahead to Stage Five, but the main focus is on saying goodbye to the past and getting together your vision of the future. Because you may not be quite clear about what that future holds, you may feel you're stepping into limbo — letting go of one trapeze before the other one is in sight. In many ways this is exactly what is happening. So it is important that you have some very clear ideas of the direction you are moving and plenty of determination to make them come to life.

• *In one company, we worked with the members of an entire department who were having trouble coming to terms with a new leader. Their previous boss had a completely different style and they had really enjoyed working for him. The new manager was trying hard to get their acceptance but they held on tightly to the memory of the past.*

In working with them all, we were able to help them see the need to complete the past and create a ritualistic ending where they could celebrate all the positive qualities of the "good old days" and at the same time say goodbye.

The following day, we helped them begin to look toward the future and create a vision of how they and their organization would be when they were all "on board" and performing enthusiastically. They were encouraged to take into the future any of the qualities from the past that they wanted. The most important factors for this group were their willingness first to let it all go — and then to turn around and look forward.

We have found in our consulting work with changing organizations that employees are usually expected to start something new without closing out the old. Little, if any, encouragement is given to say goodbye and "grieve" the loss of the way things were before they must prepare for what lies ahead. They are expected to continue with business as usual, with a strong "should line" in force.

As a result, a lot of hidden energy is put into dealing with feelings of loss while trying to perform in new ways. It generally takes longer to adjust to a new structure, new boss, or new methods of operating when the transition process is not understood or talked about.

Where You'll Find Support

There are two things happening at the same time in Stage Four and you will need to take care of both of them. First, you will need to continue consciously letting go of the past and, second, you must begin explicitly to strengthen your steps into the future.

It is important to spend time with friends and colleagues who will help you create small success-oriented projects that lead you forward and allow you to get a feel for what your new world will be like. This also may be a good time to get some specific guidance from professionals on your new situation.

Meditating or sitting quietly, imagining what your life is going to be like when "this" is all over, also will help you climb up the other side of the curve. Focusing on and perhaps updating the ideal day you wrote down at the end of Stage Three and creating a detailed vision for yourself — as described later in this chapter — will allow you to put your energy into something you want in the future. As you do, you will feel your attachment to the old situation getting weaker.

It helps to find people who have been through similar experiences and talk with them about where you've been and where you're headed. Sharing with people who understand is a wonderful way of getting some distance from the more painful parts of the transition process. You'll begin feeling as if you're back in control, although this may come and go for a while.

If your transition has to do with a job change, this is a good time to develop a mentoring relationship with someone who will support you as you take your next steps. This person could be someone who has a lot of experience in your job area or someone who cares a great deal about your success. If you can find both these characteristics in the same person, of course, that would be perfect.

How To Move On

Trusting that everything is going to work out and that you're going to be okay seems to be necessary both to letting go successfully and to moving on to the next stage. If you strengthen your trust in yourself and really believe that you have or can find everything you need to keep going — such as support, encouragement, a positive attitude, and some realistic first steps — you are likely to pass through this stage fairly quickly. Letting go of the past must be balanced with determining your vision for the future in order to move into the next stage, "testing."

At about this time in your transition, you may want to examine some of the basic beliefs you hold about yourself and your life, to see if they are still good for you.

> • *Paula had always believed that people who changed their jobs were basically unhappy, so she stayed in the same position for seven years — even though it was not exactly what she wanted. "I thought I should be grateful for what I was given, and if I made a change people would think I was dissatisfied (and that was a no-no). One day, when we were in the middle of a major reorganization at the office — and I was feeling very*

depressed — I picked up the paper and started looking at the career advertisements. Surprised at the variety of opportunities open to someone with my skills, I decided to apply for a couple of the positions. Within eight weeks I had a new job, a company car, and a bigger salary. When I look back, it's hard to believe I let myself stay so long."

Paula, like many people, was not aware of how strongly she was influenced by her old beliefs. Beliefs and assumptions usually operate outside of conscious awareness, and it takes a significant event to bring them into consciousness. (In Chapters Fourteen and Fifteen we explore how beliefs develop, what purpose they serve, and how you can change them.)

Another thing that will help you let go more easily is to develop regular exercise and relaxation habits. During Stage Three, you may have walked around feeling very tense and uptight much of the time. You probably had more headaches than usual; perhaps your neck and shoulders were stiff. Maybe you became aware of clenching your fists, grinding your teeth, aching in your lower back, or frequent stomach upsets. Whenever a big transition is under way, aches and pains such as these are not at all unusual.

Relaxation techniques and physical exercise programs are both wonderful supports for letting go of the tensions that have been held in your body while you have been coming to terms with the change. If physical tensions such as these are not released, you'll probably find it more difficult to be positive about the future; your "poor old aching" body will hold you back.

You'll find more information on relaxation techniques and exercise programs in Chapter Sixteen. For now, we suggest that you take some time out to go for a walk, read an absorbing book, or soak yourself in a lovely hot bath. You deserve it!

To further support yourself in moving on, make some decisions about things or people you need to let go of to make your load a little lighter. Are there some old letters, old photos, or old clothes you've been holding on to that could be thrown out or given away? Would a house move, or a job change help you to move forward? Maybe a change of car would release some emotional ties to the past?

> • *Joan is a friend of ours who went through a series of changes, regaining her balance only after a long period of adjustment. The last time we saw her, she told us, "The dog's dead, my husband's gone, and the kids have left home. I don't need a station wagon anymore, so I bought myself a sports car that's just for me. I feel so much brighter!"*

Stage Four is a good time to take on activities that will help you to rebuild your self-esteem. Time in "the pit" can be very draining. People are often left feeling down on themselves, since they've faced some of the darker parts of their personalities. It's important to reconnect with feelings of enthusiasm, optimism and renewed self-confidence in order to move up the other side of the curve.

> • *Graham gained over forty pounds in the first eight months after his wife left him. He felt ugly and thought people would be turned off by his appearance, so he shut himself away and only went out when he had to. He hadn't even noticed the lovely summer weather outside on the day when he decided to sort through his old school photographs. There were many of him in various sporting poses; his favorites were those showing him holding trophies for diving. Graham had always been an excellent swimmer, but he no longer had pride in his body. "I kept looking at the photographs and then looking at myself in the mirror; it was awful. At forty-one years of age I looked*

like a fat old man. I began to wonder if I had put the weight on intentionally to keep women away from me, so I couldn't get hurt again." He told us he spent the rest of that day walking by the river, developing a clear picture in his mind of how he wanted to look. He decided he no longer needed the safety of his protective layer; it was too much of a burden to take with him.

Graham joined a weight reduction program, kept an earlier photograph of himself stuck to the bathroom mirror, and started swimming again. The last we heard, he had shed the excess pounds and was enjoying a whole new social life.

Some people find new hobbies or rediscover forgotten ones, where they can be creative and feel a sense of achievement and personal well-being. Others take up running, walking, bicycling and swimming, finding that exercise really helps them to feel psychologically and physically healthier (see Chapter Sixteen). We've heard people talk about learning Aikido, T'ai Chi, and other martial arts as a way of regaining their sense of self-worth. This can be a time of great self-renewal if you're prepared to let go of the comfort of the known and seek the growth opportunities that you know are there for you.

Letting-Go: A Ritual And A Vision

You'll find the following two-part process will help you complete the process of letting go. Part One leads you through a "Letting-Go Ritual" and Part Two provides a way to create a detailed vision of your future as you'd like it to be.

Part One Letting go of the past and refocusing on the future usually happens naturally, in time. A formal ritual, however, can be valuable for gaining closure on the past and bringing the "pendulum period" to an end.

There are several steps in the ritual we use.* We suggest that you have your notebook handy as you think about each step. If you are part of a support group made up of people who are all experiencing a major transition, this ritual and the visioning process which follows in Part Two can be stimulating and useful group activities.

1. Become aware of just what it is that you now want to let go of, and write down on a piece of paper, "I now let go of ..." For example, you may want to be released from your fear of being alone, a sense of failure, a relationship with another person.

2. Close your eyes and reflect on how the person, quality or thing you are letting go helped you in the past. Give thanks for those benefits.

3. Make a very clear decision to let go of the person, quality or thing.

4. Read your statement aloud, and then burn it. The burning of your statement physicallly transforms it into a new kind of energy.

5. Again close your eyes and develop an image of the safest place you can imagine. It could be a warm sunny beach, a favorite room, or a beautiful forest. Spend a few minutes relaxing and enjoying this safe place, and know that you can return here in your imagination anytime you need to.

6. In your notebook, write the names of those people who are your closest supporters at this moment. You may wish to get in touch with them at the end of the next step, to talk about what you've been doing.

---

*Adapted from the letting go ritual developed by our friend and colleague, Ginger Swain.

Don't be surprised if you feel an overwhelming sense of sadness and loss as you complete the letting go process. You may also feel a growing emptiness and anxiety about what will fill the gap between the past and the future. You can always return to the safe place you created in Step Five above, allowing a wave of relaxation to replace the feeling of anxiety. (In Chapter Eleven we will talk about the process of "systematic desensitization" in more detail.)

You have done more work than you might think by going through the ritual in Part One, and you need to give this work a chance to sink in before going on to Part Two, which shifts your focus to the future. Take at least a couple of hours' break. Some people like to go for a walk, others prefer to sleep on it overnight — perhaps recording their dreams the next morning.

Part Two Having completed the Letting Go Ritual, it is time to be very detailed about how you want your new situation to unfold. The reason is to give you something specific to look forward to — something you have created for yourself. Having a vision of the future, you will naturally begin to look for people and situations that can lead you to what you want. Without specifying a vision, you are at best likely to get haphazard results and may even drift back into holding on to the past.

As a way of moving on from Stage Three, we asked you in the last chapter to envision an ideal day for yourself, to help you begin to create the future you would really like to have. Now, it's time to take this another step and become much more specific about what you want.

Spend a few minutes with your eyes closed — some people find it easier to do this with some background music playing — thinking about how your life would be if it could be exactly the way you want it a year or two from now. Then take about ten minutes to think about your answers to the questions below.

If you could have things exactly the way you want them:

How do you look and feel physically? How much do you weigh? How fit are you?

How are you stretching your mind? What new knowledge and skills are you acquiring?

How are you dealing with your feelings? Are you open to expressing them? What is your emotional outlook?

What are the things that inspire you? Is it your work, nature, music?

How are your relationships with your family, friends and colleagues?

What have been some of your recent achievements (one or two years from now)? What are you proud of?

What "things" do you have around you? What is your house like? Your car? What other material possessions do you have?

Do you have any special interests and hobbies? What are they?

What is your ideal day at work (one or two years from now)? What is the work you are doing? What are your surroundings like? How are your relationships with your colleagues? How does it feel to work there?

Take a few moments to write down your answers in your journal or notebook. You will have the greatest success (and the most fun!) if you write as if it's all already true. That is, imagine that it really is one or two years from now and you're describing your life at that moment. Use the present tense "I am...," "I have..." and "I choose..." and NOT the future tense of "I want..." "I will..." or "I should..." Writing in the present tense seems to have much more power to influence your attitude change and can help you get what you want for yourself more efficiently.

You'll find it very interesting now to compare this ideal day with the one you created at the end of Stage Three. You probably are feeling better about things now than you did in "the pit," and you're probably able to be more specific about what you want in the future. Plan to work with this vision from time to time and change it as you go along. The "self-fulfilling prophecy" works much better when you keep on *re-visioning,* rather than thinking of it as something you do only once.

Common Areas Of Confusion	Suggested Affirmations
Can I trust myself? Do I have enough courage?	*I can do it. I've succeeded before.*
Do I have the skills and knowledge to move ahead?	*I have skills and knowledge and I know how to acquire more if needed.*
Will I be able to get on with things now?	*I am ready.*
Will I fit in? Will I be accepted?	*I accept myself. I know there's a place for me.*

Key Growth Opportunity: Turning around to face the future and experiencing a sense of renewed self-confidence and optimism.

Personal Notes On Stage Four

- Write down anything you are holding onto that you really need to let go of so you can move into the future. What are some steps you have taken in the past that have helped you let go of unwanted thoughts and feelings?
- Think about your support system and the people you know. Can you think of any relationships that are holding you back, that you need to let go of? If so, who are they? What are some first steps you can take to change or end these relationships? Is there anyone you need to forgive?
- Are there any new relationships you need to form in order to help you move forward? If so, who are the people? What are some first steps you can take to begin building these relationships?
- Is there anything else you can do to help you move forward? Are you holding onto old letters and photographs that you need to let go of (or maybe put away in a safe place)?

Are You Ready for Stage Five?

By now you should be feeling a sense of completion of the past and excitement about the future. You're getting anxious to get back in the swing of things, eager to "show off" your growing experience of self-determination.

There may still be some feelings of uncertainty, but you find it easy to quiet them and they don't last for very long. You're eager to try out something new and different; you wake up in the morning raring to go!

8

STAGE FIVE:
TESTING THE LIMITS

One step at a time, or shall I rush in?
I have to be a big hit.
I know I can do it, it's time to begin!
I'm excited, I have to admit.

As you let go of the past situation and face the future with a growing sense of self-confidence, you will begin experiencing a stronger drive for making the change. Holding on traps a lot of energy. Letting Go releases that energy, in the form of enthusiasm, optimism, and physical vitality as you free yourself from the old situation and look forward to the opportunities the future has to offer.

As the future gets brighter and you know that you're going to make it after all, you'll feel a growing need to move on and to be accepted by others in your new reality or role. This will lead you to want to be more active and to try out your new wings. Don't be surprised, however, if you find yourself being more impulsive than you've ever been and eager to dive into every opportunity you can find to push the limits and prove yourself.

This Testing Stage allows you to strengthen the foundation of the new situation so that you begin to feel more secure and more optimistic about the future. It is also a time for taking bigger risks — and for celebrating successes you have had in your new world.

What It's Like

As is suggested by its name, the Testing Stage is one where you'll want to try out new things. You'll feel your energy coming back more and more each day. There will be lots of trials and lots of errors. You'll certainly experience some successes that will move you forward and build your confidence, and some failures that may temporarily push you back to the previous stage. The more small successes you can create for yourself at this time, the better.

   • *In his new job as a salesperson, Paul had to set his own monthly sales targets for review with his boss. He had spent the night before working them through and presented them proudly the next day. His boss was very impressed but felt they were a little over-ambitious. He suggested that Paul be a little more realistic, but Paul was very excited, and convinced he could do it.*

   The first week he met the target and on the Friday evening brought in a bottle of champagne to share with his colleagues. The second week he was only a little short of the sales target, but felt sure that he could make it up by the end of the month. However, it became more difficult each week and by the end of the first month he was twenty-five percent below his monthly target. He was disappointed and began to question whether he should have stayed in his previous job. His boss, happily, had seen it all before and knew that this was just a phase as new salespeople tested their mettle in the marketplace. He congratulated Paul for his willingness to take the risk and quickly helped him regain his self-esteem.

As you experiment and build your confidence, it is important to remain aware of how your energy and activity may appear to others close to you. People in this stage often come across as missionaries, giving off a sense of being invincible. They may even try to get everyone to do the same thing because it's so great! In the seventies, a lot of people went through life-changing training programs: Some assertiveness training, encounter groups, est, sensitivity training, transcendental meditation.... trainees later put a lot of energy into trying to convert others to see things their way, or at the very least to attend the program.

You may feel a sense of urgency during this testing stage. It seems as if it's time to get on with things, and you may give the impression of cockiness and bravado which others find difficult to be around. It's important that you are aware of this very natural tendency in Stage Five, so that you can make amends whenever you notice — or are told — that it's happening.

Another feature of this stage is that some people tend to become "larger than life" in whatever their new situation is.

• *At a recent professional gathering of about seventy people, all the participants introduced themselves. When it was her turn, a wonderful friend of ours didn't give her name. Instead, she stood with her hands under her swollen tummy and a big smile on her face, and said, "I'm pregnant!"*

This is a time when you may act out your stereotyped understanding of the role into which you're moving. People who have recently divorced begin to do what they think single people do, and they may do it in a highly exaggerated way for a while. People who are moving into a new job may begin to dress and act the part. Someone who has just become an engineer, a trainer, or a flight attendant, is likely to wear "the uniform," use the jargon and spend as much time as possible "hanging out" with others in the field — activities which are likely to help one feel a part of a new career world.

All of this is an important part of moving through the transition curve because it takes you from thinking about what it will be like in the new situation, to actually living it out. It can also be a time of fun and playfulness, as any painful memories take their place in the past, and your focus is very clearly rooted in today. Don't be too surprised, however, if you get occasional "flashbacks" of the way it used to be. It can take a little time before you'll fully live in the "new."

One final characteristic typical of this stage is that most people are a little more outgoing than may be usual for them. Some people find it important to make sure people know who they are, while others are driven by the need to prove how capable and competent they are. Some get involved in any and every activity imaginable, while others join only a few selected groups in search of a sense of belonging.

Where You'll Find Support

One of the best ways to support yourself through this exciting stage is to remain clear about the results you want most from your transition and to move toward them one step at a time. In the early days, you want to gather a lot of small successes to build your confidence — any failure from taking too big a risk can set you back quite a bit.

Other people tend to be very important to someone going through this stage. Others can serve a "mentoring" role here, helping you explore some of your alternatives and engaging in post-mortems with you, so that you can learn as much as possible from each step. You can help yourself do this also, by keeping a daily journal and reviewing it from time to time.

People frequently need to receive encouragement that they're on the right track. Many people find that they can learn the most when they are trying things out, encouraging others to give them feedback along the way.

You'll most likely want to spend time with others who have the same interests and speak the same "language" you do. When people divorce, for instance, they begin to have less in common with their married friends and often elect to join in more frequently with others who are single. Likewise, those who lose a spouse will tend to find others in the same situation. If you've taken on a new job, you will likely look for support from your new colleagues — and may find it more difficult to be with your old ones.

How To Move On

As you test the boundaries, both your own and those of the new situation, you'll find what works for you and what doesn't. Once this is done, you can choose to act in ways that make things work out as you want them to.

The following activity will help you get a clearer idea of what qualities are present whenever you're successful, whether at work, in a relationship, in studying, or in living every day the way you want it to be. It turns out that everyone can identify those unique personal qualities that must be present in order to make sure they are successful. This activity helps you to discover your own "peak performance qualities."

• First of all, think of three times when you were really pleased with yourself — something you helped to make happen that made you feel very good about yourself and what you achieved. They can be stories from your school days: being part of a team; passing exams; a part in the school play. They can be stories from work: completing an important project; earning a promotion. They can be stories from your social or family life: planning a surprise birthday party; making a successful house move; finding the ideal partner.

Choose three situations that were real highlights for you. They don't have to be recent, but you must have enough information so that you can describe in detail what happened at the beginning, middle and end.

• Using your notebook or journal, write down enough detail from each of the three experiences so that someone else would be able to understand completely what it is you are describing.

Story 1.

Story 2.

Story 3.

• Now look over your stories and pick out the characteristics and qualities that are present in every story, and write them down. Perhaps a friend could help you. Everyone has some unique characteristics and qualities *always* present when they have a success experience.

Some examples might be that you always did some *planning;* you always kept a *clear goal* in mind; you were helped by your *spirit of adventure* or sense of *challenge;* you relied on your *creativity;* or you were always in *control.*

My key qualities for success:

• Now that you know what these qualities are, you can make sure that you use them when you start something else new. If you don't, you probably won't get the best results.

Take a moment and place a check mark beside all those key qualities that are already present in your new situation, and make a note of anything more you may need to do to make sure you can use them. For example, if you found in your stories that you always had a good grasp of the big picture, and you feel you already have a good sense of the big picture in your transition, you might decide to spend a moment each morning thinking about it and changing it as needed.

Also, do a little planning about how to bring into play any of your unique qualities absent in your new situation. For example, if you found you had a "spirit of adventure" in all of your stories, and you're feeling a lot of drudgery in your transition, how can you switch some of your energy into an "adventurous" project?

By being aware of your unique success qualities, you'll find it easier to recognize opportunities where you can use them. You'll probably remember a time when you had a heightened awareness of something — a place, a car, an event — and then, "like magic," you noticed that it kept being mentioned, or you read about it in the paper, or you saw many more of them than before. Once you become more aware or conscious of something, you are much more sensitive to it in your environment. The same is true of success qualities. The more aware you are of them, the more you'll know how to build them regularly into your activities.

You know you're nearing the completion of this stage when you begin to feel more relaxed. Now you can enjoy sitting back and shifting your focus gradually toward a deeper understanding of just what the transition is all about. Anything that helps you to broaden your perspective and deepen your understanding will help you move ahead.

One way to do this is to read books or other materials related to your transition. There is a list of books and other resources in the Appendix you'll find useful. Many people at this stage enjoy reading about others' experiences during similar transitions. They may have found it impossible to concentrate on reading anything of substance before this time because their energy has been devoted to survival.

Typical Areas Of Confusion	Suggested Affirmations
Do they really like and respect me?	I am respected and liked.
Am I doing as well as I can?	I am on my way.
Is this really what I want to be doing?	I am building my future. I am doing the right thing for myself at this time.
Am I gaining respect?	I am making a contribution worthy of respect.

Key Growth Opportunity: Strengthening self-confidence and gaining experience in your new world.

Personal Notes On Stage Five
- Think of other small or big changes you have made. How have you tested yourself in those situations? Do you remember what worked well for you and what didn't?
- What are some things you need to be doing, more or less, to help you move on?
- As you think of your present support network, who can be most helpful to you in this stage? Who are the people who help you to identify alternatives, tell you when you're going overboard, help you to stay optimistic, and like to have fun with you?

Are You Ready for Stage Six?
Are you feeling a need to reflect quietly on all that has been happening in order to put it into perspective? By now you will be feeling as if everything is falling into place. You're interested in understanding what this experience has meant and what you have learned from it all.

9

STAGE SIX:
SEARCHING FOR
MEANING

The choice is mine to grow or live,
to share the gifts I have to give,
to make a difference as I roam,
finding peace on my way home.

After the stages of confusion and uncertainty comes a growing desire for order and a sense of stability. It is now that you're likely to want to look back and review what has happened to you throughout the entire transition process.

In his book *Illusions,* Richard Bach says, "There's no such thing as a problem without a gift for you in its hands." This then is a time to step back, to get off the emotional roller coaster and get a deeper understanding — perhaps on a more spiritual level — of exactly what the change and the experiences have meant. It is also a time for gaining new perspectives about yourself, your role, and the very nature of being human.

People we've worked with find they need this stage to slow down the pace, take a look at where they've been, where they are now, and where they want to go. It's a time for pulling out the pearls of wisdom found during the journey; a time to gather the treasures and reap the rewards that come with going through a major life change. It's the calm after the storm, a "healing time" after some of the "craziness" that may have come with the questioning, letting go, and testing stages.

You will also find yourself wanting to understand what exactly has happened and why, to glean all the richness and the learning from your experiences. This time of searching out the meaning also helps you get the information you'll need for future decisions having to do with the change, as well as helping you build a clearer idea about your purpose.

What It's Like

It is likely that you'll find yourself feeling a greater sense of inner peace, with only the occasional memory of the "darker days." The most common experience at this point of the curve is feeling as if everything's in place and you're going to be fine. You'll begin to realize that it was all worth it, to feel wiser and more "whole" than before, as well as more grounded and back in control.

As the desire to understand grows, you probably will want gain more knowledge about the bigger world, in an attempt to identify how you can make a difference with what you've learned and whom you've become. You may also want to seek out someone who will help you get a clearer picture about your next steps.

One of the characteristics of the early part of this stage is that people tend to be less active than in Stage Five and spend more time alone, often looking inside themselves for some deeper answers to questions about life's meaning. (Chapter Seventeen includes a detailed step-by-step process for identifying or clarifying your life purpose.)

In many ways, Stage Six is the time when all the upheaval makes sense for the first time, as you are now able to look at the whole picture. Even though your focus is inward, you'll probably experience yourself as being part of the bigger human family. It is now that the term "alone" does not mean "lonely" but more "all-one." The feeling of separateness that you probably knew only too well in the Stage Three is now accepted as being true only on the physical level.

It's in this stage also that you'll probably want to help others through the same process. It is often a time when people want to give back some of the learning they've gained along the way. Recovering alcoholics help others heal their disease; people who have divorced spend time with others who are going through the process; people who have succeeded in making a career change help others do the same; and those who retire encourage others to make the most of their new freedom and help them up the other side of the curve.

> • *Angela had been living with cancer and had reached a point where she had come to terms with her illness. Even with support groups she had found it very difficult to accept this life-threatening disease and had spent several months going up and down through the pendulum period of the transition process.*
>
> *As she began to understand what her illness actually meant to her, she decided that she wanted to help others. So she began spending time with those who had just learned that they had cancer, comforting them and being available whenever they needed her. She said it gave her a whole new reason for living.*

Some people write books, plays, poetry or music about their journeys as a way of helping others make similar adjustments. It's a wonderful way of coming to terms with your transition and finding out what really happened! You don't have to write a bestseller — it will help just to make a journal entry on your understanding of exactly what you've been through.

For many people, this stage provides the opportunity to get in touch with the meaning of their lives, their relationships and their work, and to celebrate the courage it takes to

Where You'll Find Support

Sitting quietly meditating, watching a sunrise or sunset, or just listening to music are wonderful supports at this stage. For some people this can be difficult because our society sends out such a strong message about keeping busy by "doing" things that people often feel guilty just "being" with themselves.

If this is true for you, and you need a good reason to take time for yourself, then tell yourself that by having these few moments of quiet you'll be much better at whatever it is you have to do. If sitting and doing nothing is not your style, then another way of supporting yourself in this stage is by spending some time with nature. You can go for a walk, go to the beach or a city park, go fishing, go canoeing, or go for a bike ride. Just use this time for thinking about yourself and your life.

Anytime you need more understanding of, or a deeper meaning for, your life, we recommend a walk in nature, away from the concrete and the cars. Many people have to go through a major life transition to get back in touch with themselves and rediscover what life is all about.

Once more, keeping a journal or a log of your thoughts and feelings is a useful way of staying in touch with your inner process. You may want to continue this after the transition is over.

How To Move On

It is now that you may choose to take part in some seminars to get some new skills and also to share your experiences. You'll probably find yourself developing new friendships that support you in the direction you are heading.

Some people rediscover old hobbies and pastimes, or begin new ones that they've always thought about doing. It may also be that you reconnect with old friends and feel a renewed sense of being alive and wanting to "play" again — taking life less seriously.

One thing for sure, you'll have a growing sense of peace as you move on to the next stage: Integration.

Typical Areas Of Confusion	Suggested Affirmations
Can I really make a difference?	*What I have to give is worthwhile and valuable.*
Will I be able to learn enough quickly enough?	*I have plenty of time and I'm learning.*
What do I want to do next?	*I will find what I'm looking for.*
Is this where I really belong?	*I am respected and I belong here.*

Key Growth Opportunity: Understanding how change and transition helps us grow and get in touch with the deeper meaning of our lives.

Personal Notes On Stage Six

- When you look back at how you have moved through this transition, what do you really value about yourself?
- In your life as a whole what do you really enjoy about being you?
- What matters to you so much that you would take a stand for it?
- Is there anything you need to add, or change about the vision you wrote for yourself in Stage Four?
- What do you need to do NOW to help your vision come to life?

Make a list of the specific steps you need to take and the habits you need to change or establish. What can you do today?

Are You Ready for Stage Seven?

If you feel you have a good grasp of what you've been through, have been able to share it, and have a good understanding of what it's all meant, you're ready to move on. You'll feel a growing sense of inner peace and quiet and begin to focus very clearly on the present and the future.

10

STAGE SEVEN: *INTEGRATING*

I'm home again at last.
the storm of change has passed,
and though my searching will not cease.
I'll treasure this sweet moment's peace.

As your commitment to life deepens, you learn to look at everything that has happened as having meaning, and see its importance in bringing you to where you are now. The term "integration" is really the final "letting go," and is a time for completely accepting all that has happened and then moving on to your life's next steps.

At this time, you'll begin to refer to the transition or change as something that has passed. It's no longer a part of your everyday thinking, but something you have added to your collection of life experiences.

This stage is critical to the overall transition process because it provides you with the opportunity to pull everything together and to complete this passage. After looking back at what you learned in Stage Six, you can now use everything you picked up along the way to help you today and in the future. Integrating your learning experience will make you stronger, more aware and more prepared for living every moment fully. It is a time also to rest up for a while, and to enjoy a sense of well-being. Although in many ways this stage is the "last" one, it is also the one that comes before the next transition!

What It's Like

You'll no longer feel the sense of struggling with different parts of yourself that you may have found in nearly all of the earlier stages. You'll cease thinking so frequently about what has happened and no longer feel so attached to it. Once you have recognized that it was worth every moment — even though at times it may not have seemed that way — you may go days or weeks without thinking about "it."

As a sense of peace and meaning replaces the uncertainty of the recent past, you'll certainly want to get on with your life. You are ready to step out and make a difference — maybe on a completely different path than the one you were on before the transition. Or you might just feel "older and wiser" and be open to whatever comes your way. Whatever your choice, there is a feeling of balance and harmony; you may have had moments of these along the way, but now they are present for longer periods as you go about your daily activities.

You will feel much more confident and happy with people again — sometimes sharing your experience if you think it will help them. If your change has been a marriage, you will feel at ease with your mate; if it has been a divorce, you will be more at ease with being on your own or moving into another relationship; if you have moved to a new job, you will be feeling more capable of achieving the task; if you have retired, you'll no longer be wondering what to do with yourself and probably be finding it hard to understand how you ever had time for work; if you have lost someone close to you, you'll treasure your memory and be fully alive in the present.

• *Jack and Sally both lost their only surviving parents (his mother, her father) within a two-month period. They had difficult times coming to terms with their losses, and also with sorting out the details of selling of houses and everything else. They told us: "It was a tough two years but we learned a lot about ourselves and each other. We both feel much more mature, and at the same time have become more playful and less serious about life. It's not that we don't miss them, but it's time for us to look forward. We've even planned to take four weeks off work and tour the country. We really feel we deserve it."*

At this stage, it is important that you view the transition as completed. It's also important not to get carried away by an illusion that things will be stable forever. They may be for a while, but nature has a wonderful way of making sure that everything doesn't happen all at once, and — if you are to continue growing — it's probably a good idea to accept that this too is just a stage. It is essential for completing the present transition, but probably is only a breathing space before the beginning of the next big one. This doesn't mean that you have to think about going out and stirring up a new change, of course. Rest for a while, and enjoy the sense of fulfillment and new growth. It may be two or three years before you feel the need to start a new journey. You still have a lot of exploring to do in your new situation.

Learning at this stage is an ongoing celebration of new discoveries. Some small, some big, but rarely painful. It's like the seed that, having survived the winter, has sprouted, pushing its way above the ground and blossoming. Now it is enjoying the sunshine, observing the bees and discovering how to stay bright even on wet and windy days.

Emotionally you'll feel at ease with yourself, you'll be back in control and unafraid to allow feelings of joy and sadness to come and go. You'll understand the value of your moods and be able to see that they help you to get the richness out of every moment; like the "seven dwarfs," all have a role to play.

Where You'll Find Support

This is a time for making existing relationships even deeper and for building some new ones. It's a time for relaxing and enjoying each day as it comes.

Those around you will continue to be valuable supporters, and you will find that you no longer need them to approve of you. You're able to enjoy them for who they are, regardless of whether they see the world the same as you. You have become more self-assured and inner-directed.

You will face each new challenge with an open mind and a sense of curiosity. People will be a source of inspiration and you will be able to hear them much more clearly, now that your own inner dialogue has quieted.

You'll find it supportive to incorporate some kind of daily relaxation and exercise habit into your life. It's time to have fun and let the child in you come out to play. You've been on a great adventure and you have some scars to prove it. Now that they're all healed up, you feel a sense of pride and accomplishment.

- *Chris, a father of two, was only forty-three years old when he suffered a major heart attack. At first, he couldn't believe it and thought it was all a terrible nightmare. Then he grew more and more angry — "why me?" He knew others who were far heavier and smoked twice as much as he did!*

When he recognized the many changes he would have to make to his lifestyle, he sank into a feeling of despair, wondering whether life would be worth living. After a while, he began to question his priorities and some deeper beliefs, and within a couple of months began to believe he could make the needed changes.

He read books, experimented with cooking, and started walking a couple of miles a day. He realized how lucky he was and how he'd been given a "second chance."

"I no longer take things for granted anymore; the sunrise and the sunset, the changing seasons are magic. I have found a new meaning to my life and am no longer driven by my desire to climb the corporate ladder. I really didn't see my children grow up, so now I rarely work late and my weekends are sacred family time. Each day is a new experience and I feel grateful for having the opportunity to clean up my act before it was too late. Interestingly, my performance at work has actually improved; I seem to be able to get more done in less time. Funny isn't it?

"I'm not exactly sure what the future holds but I know I'll be healthier at fifty than I was at forty. In fact, I probably already am and it's only taken eighteen months. I guess I'm one of the lucky ones. I got an early wake up call."

How To Move On

This is a good opportunity for taking one final look at all you have learned as you have moved through the seven stages of transition, and what it means as you move into the future.

• What have been the greatest rewards for you as a result of this change that you are taking with you into the future? More responsibility? Greater self-awareness? Personal freedom?

- What is it that you are now doing that this transition has opened for you?
- If a good friend or relative hadn't seen you for several years and met you now what would they say? "You've changed, you're so much more ..."
- Finally, find some colored pencils and using words, pictures and colors, describe your life's journey, where you've been and where you're headed. You may prefer to find a large sheet of paper and make a poster. Don't worry about your artistic ability; it's for you, so enjoy yourself!

Suggested Affirmations

I am responsible for my choices.

There are things I have learned that will be valuable to others.

I am ready for my next challenge.

I am where I need to be.

Key Growth Opportunity: Seeing the deeper meaning in all things and recognizing the courage it takes to reach beyond the boundaries of what's safe and familiar.

Are You Ready For....?

You are likely to feel very well grounded in the present with a very clear picture of where you are heading. The future looks very bright and you are excited about life and its meaning.

You feel it is time to expand your horizons and are unafraid to step out and take a risk, because you feel very secure in yourself. You know that complacency is to be steered clear of at this stage of the transition and you continue to put energy into your vision.

In time, when you no longer feel you are growing or you need a new challenge, you will have to make some choices about future changes, but for now take time to celebrate being alive.

COMMONLY ASKED QUESTIONS
ABOUT THE LIFE CHANGES CURVE

Can I avoid stage three?

This is probably one of the most frequently asked questions and the answer is, "Yes ..... BUT...." Those people who do avoid "the pit" usually get stuck in the earlier stage of denial and minimization. Others who have tried to rush through "the pit" after a major life change have found themselves experiencing this stage very intensely when they face the next transition. The deeper questions, about life and its meaning, about coming to terms with the shadow side of our human nature, have to be dealt with sooner or later. If you do avoid this admittedly difficult stage during one time through the curve you may have a double dose next time around.

As mentioned in Chapter Three, the intensity of your experience will depend on a number of factors: how much the change takes you by surprise; your life stage; the number of other changes you are experiencing. For some people Stage Three may be relatively short-lived, whereas others will remember it for the rest of their lives. In any event, we don't recommend skipping it; this questioning and struggle with yourself can result in much growth in wisdom and self-esteem.

Is it possible to go through the whole curve in only a few days?

It sure is, and many people do when they are dealing with minor transitions. You may even find yourself experiencing all of the seven stages in a matter of hours when you lock your keys in the car, lose your wallet, or when your bags don't arrive on the carousel at the airport!

However if you are facing a significant life change the adjustment process will take much longer. Some people have told us of speeding along the curve in the first few days of a change, and then going through a more prolonged experience of the remaining stages in the months that followed.

Do I have to experience all the stages?

It is unlikely that you'll be able to avoid any of the stages, although you may not move through the curve in linear fashion. You may also find yourself acutely aware of one stage and hardly noticing another. Again, this will depend on your earlier transition experiences as well as other factors described in Chapter Three.

If there were one thing I could do to help myself through the curve, what would it be?

Perhaps the most valuable asset you can have to make the transition adjustment easier is a good support network — and the courage to use it. Many people when they are confused or in pain try to go it alone; the experience can be much less fearful by sharing what's going on with a trusted friend. Even people who are introverted by nature find that turning to someone who will listen and care for them makes the tougher times a little easier.

Supporting yourself by looking after your physical health can also make a big difference in how you experience a life change. In Stages Three and Four especially it is a good idea to continue to exercise and relax on a regular basis, as well as keeping an eye on what you eat.

What can I do to help someone who is stuck in stage three?

You can start by deciding whether the person is really "stuck," or just doing a lot of soul searching (looking over the description in Chapter Six may help you to decide). There are really no magic recipes here, and people won't move until they're ready to. Some may even choose to stay in "the pit" for years.

Someone who's really stuck, seeing only the dark side of the situation after several months, may be helped by considering the following four questions:

• What's the immediate problem and what can you do about it right now?

• If things continue this way, what do you predict will happen?

• Is there a new way you could approach things?

• If someone gave you a magic wand to create your perfect future, how could you make it?

It's a good idea to ask these questions in this order because it focuses the person first on the known and familiar situation, then gently guides him or her into a more creative way of looking at things. Don't be surprised if the answers are a little confused or even uninteresting at first. The most important thing is to ask the questions so that the person begins to think about some possible alternatives. If you just listen, with genuine caring and concern, you'll be helping enormously.

What if I'm going through more than one transition at the same time?

This is often the case, as one major life change usually triggers others. It is not uncommon for people to go through multiple transitions at the same time and feel as if they're all mixed in together. It can make these times a lot easier if you draw separate curves for each of the transitions and identify where you are on each, as shown on the next page.

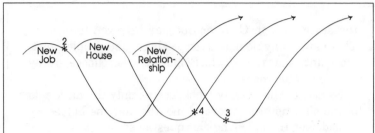

For example, you might be in Stage Two in regard to
your new job, Stage Four in settling in your new home and
neighborhood, and the relationship you've recently started
may have you right down in the bottom of Stage Three,
questioning whether you really need this on top of all the
other changes in your life!

Can I be in stage four or five and drop back into stage three?

Yes, you can, and a lot of people do. This is why we call
it "the pendulum period!" It is very common for people to
feel they have met all the monsters only to come face to
face with yet another one. Stage Four is a time of healing
and forgiveness and you are likely to still have a foot in
both worlds. You've decided to go up the other side but
there's still some repair work to do and some loose ends to
tie up in the situation you are leaving behind. You've
invested a lot of energy in "what used to be," so it isn't going
to let you go without a struggle.

In Stage Five you may find yourself revisiting the pit if
you face a setback in your "new world." You may have a
little more work to do before you can really get going on
your way.

What are the most important things to remember when I'm in the middle of yet another transition?

This is a very big question. This book provides you with
many different and practical suggestions that will help you

through the transition experience. Perhaps the best way to answer this right now is on a philosophical level. Often when people are faced with a major life change they lose sight of the larger meaning of their lives — their sense of universal purpose. This can lead to feelings of powerlessness and despair, and a loss of will to live and to learn.

Holding on to the belief that what is happening is neither accidental nor haphazard in the bigger picture of your life will help you learn most from your experiences. Take on the role of an explorer and adventurer and discard that of "innocent victim." From time to time you are bound to question and doubt all that you hold to be true; this too is an important part of the journey not to be rushed or made light of. Loving yourself unconditionally at every step along the way will make the life change experience more like a treasure hunt — although the riches may be disguised in unusual ways.

A FAMILY OF FOUR

Barbara and Terry had three children, twin boys aged ten, and a little girl named Grace. In the summer of her eighth birthday Grace started complaining about being more tired than usual; she seemed less of a tomboy, sitting off to the side rather than playing with her brothers. At first, her parents weren't too worried, but when she began to complain of pain from time to time, Barbara took her to a physician.

It wasn't long before the results of Grace's blood tests showed that she had leukemia. When Barbara and Terry were first told, they remember just staring at each other. Then Terry, who was convinced there had been a mistake, insisted that the doctor check to be sure that the blood hadn't been mixed up in any way. The results came back the same.

They described the first couple of months as like existing on remote control. "We thought we were doing great. People would ask us how we were and we'd say 'Just fine, everything's going to work out perfectly.' " Occasionally, they both admitted to feeling very sad, but they wouldn't show it because they felt they needed to be strong for each other.

Meanwhile, encouraged by all the research and the high cure rate of this kind of cancer in children, Barbara and Terry continued as if everything were normal. They had decided not to tell the boys how sick Grace really was, and they continued to tell her that she would soon be better.

Barbara tells what happened next:

"We had a wonderful vacation that summer. We didn't even consider that it would be the last one we'd have as a complete family. Grace's health was deteriorating, but we didn't want to accept it and kept trying to convince each other that there were signs of improvement.

"By winter that year, she was getting up only for a few hours a day and we were still pretending she was going to get better. We weren't going to give up for anything. Then one day the doctor told us that she didn't have much longer — one, maybe two, months. It was devastating. We went to bed that night and got so mad with God for doing this to us. It wasn't fair; she was so small and vulnerable and had hardly lived. We even offered our own lives if He would save her. 'Why, why, why?' That's all we kept asking! The next weeks were awful. We tried to keep up a strong appearance, but we were both broken up inside and after the kids were all asleep we'd cry. And then get angry with the doctors, the treatment, and with death for wanting to take our little girl away.

"What was interesting for our marriage was that when we were trying to protect each other, we discovered that we were both desperately lonely. It was only when we began to let our feelings out that we could help each other — and then we felt so close! It was probably the closest we'd ever been in our fifteen years together.

"It was such a beautiful day when she died. It was early spring and the sky and the air were so clear. The smells of the blossoms were out of this world — we'd never smelled anything like it before and only one time since, and that was on the second anniversary of her death.

"We both cried a lot at her funeral and that helped the boys because they knew it was okay for them to cry too. They had a really tough time for the couple of months following, but they helped each other a great deal and we all talked about it openly. After the wake, we went for a long walk in the mountains, in some ways relieved it was all over. She wasn't in pain anymore and we knew she would be looked after. It was a very special walk and, though it may sound strange, we were both convinced she was with us in some way.

"It wasn't until late summer that we could bring ourselves to give her clothes away. We'd left her room exactly as it was — I suppose just in case she came back. But we knew she wasn't going to, and we started to make some new plans for the layout of the house. From time to time, we'd feel weepy or snap at each other, but the really tough times were behind us.

"We had a special Christmas card made that year that said, 'From the Four Of Us!' We started looking for all the advantages of being only four, and there were many. We even suggested to friends who were thinking of having children that they stop after two kids. It was all a little weird when we look back at it but, I think it was important for us as a family."

Terry continued:

"Two years after Grace died, we had a memorial service. We sat for hours and hours talking about what a beautiful child she had been and the hundreds of gifts she had brought into our lives. Even her illness had been a gift in some ways. We learned to see life completely differently; now we treasure every single second of it — there are no guarantees. When your child dies, it's very different than when an older person dies. Your children are supposed to outlive you! It sure wakes you up to the fact that death has no respect for age.

"Another gift she gave to us was each other. I think we were just drifting along in our marriage, the way that a lot of folks do. Now we really take time to be with each other; we don't live so much on the surface anymore. We're thinking of putting together a support group for people who are going through what happened to us; we know it can tear you apart. We got closer to each other, but we've heard a lot of stories in which the husband and wife divorce after they lose a child. That must be a double blow. We can see how it could happen but it doesn't have to, not if you see the bigger picture. We both believe very strongly in a world beyond this one and that Grace is safe. She was only here for a while to learn something for herself and to be a teacher to us."

The last we heard from Barbara and Terry was that they were taking a family trip to Europe before the boys started their freshman year at high school. Grace was still with them in many ways and they occasionally wondered if there was anything more they could have done. They thought about having another child, but decided to remain 'a family of four.' "

PART THREE

MAKING THE MOST
OF IT ALL

11

HOW TO
MAKE IT EASIER

In this chapter we'll help you to find out what you need to know to make the transition a little easier. Sadly, there are no guarantees, but some of these ideas may help you through the tougher times.

First, as early as possible in your transition process, find out as much as you can about the way you've handled changes in the past. Second, be clear about where you want to end up after the change is over. This won't necessarily stop you from feeling afraid and alone from time to time, but it will make the darker days much easier to handle.

Looking Back

Once again, you'll need your life change notebook as you work with this chapter.

Your experiences as you've dealt with earlier changes are among the best sources of information you have.

1. Under the heading of "My Past Experiences," list *all* the changes you can remember in your life. They can be small or big ones and can come from as far back as you can remember. For example, your first day at a new school; when your family moved to a different house; the death of a grandparent; the break up of a close friendship; graduating from high shcool; your first job; and any others you can remember.

2. Now place check marks next to four or five significant changes, such as those that were hardest to come to terms with, those in which you felt angry or hurt, and those in which your reaction to the change surprised you.

3. Thinking just about the four or five changes you checked in step 2, write down the feelings you had and how you looked after yourself. Did you reach out to friends or spend lots of time on your own?

4. Looking over your notes, are there any similarities or common patterns of thoughts and feelings? How did you help yourself through these changes?

5. Is there anything you did then that you don't want to do again?

6. Is there anything more you could be doing now to help yourself with your current transition?

You've been through many changes before and survived, and now that you've recalled some of your successes, this one may be a little easier to handle. Examining how you've dealt with life changes in the past will give you an idea of some of your own earlier patterns of transition and what you need to watch out for. Some people have found that their patterns lead them to really doubt themselves and withdraw from the world — only to realize afterwards that they would have had an easier time if they had asked for some help along the way.

Among the most common patterns we find are anger and hurt; withdrawal and "stiff upper lip"; confusion and fear of the unknown; and sadness and worry. Knowing that you tend to have a particular pattern can be helpful. Also, if you know what your emotional response is likely to be, you can help yourself (and others!) be ready for it the next time it happens.

Looking Ahead

Whether the change is one you chose for yourself or one that was imposed on you, it helps to get a clear idea of what you want at the end of the road.

> • *Sandra had been left by her husband after twenty years of marriage and had a hard time imagining what it would be like to be single again. She spent many months mourning the loss; then, with the help of some of her friends and some time alone, she was able to develop a clear picture of how she could be living her life more fully once the divorce was final. She explored many long-latent interests, envisioned herself actively involved in the community, and even began to get quite excited about dating again.*
>
> *Sandra had always been an adventurer at heart and had "clipped her wings" when she got married. Traveling always appealed to her and she soon saw that there was nothing to stop her from going anywhere in the world. She began thinking about taking a trip to India and Tibet, maybe going through Europe on the way. As her excitement grew and she got a clearer picture of exactly what she wanted, things started to happen as if by magic.*

*She found a sponsor who paid for her to attend photog-
raphy classes so she could develop a pictorial exhibit of
her journey to the Himalayas. She got offers of accom-
modation quite out of the blue and a friend of hers "just
happened" to be able to house sit until she came back.
"Sure there were some risks involved," she told us, "but
when you really know what will make your life meaning-
ful, you have to follow your dreams."*

In the early stages of a transition, it isn't always easy to
think about the future, because a lot of your energy is being
put into surviving one day at a time. But if you can think
ahead for a moment, imagine that the change you are currently most concerned about is now over and you're up the other
side of it. Dream a little in your notebook:

1. Under the heading of "My Ideal Outcome," write
down what you imagine you will be doing and how you
will be feeling after the change is over, if everything
works out ideally. Let yourself go. Pretend that you
have that magic wand.

2. Is there anything you haven't written down
because you really don't believe you can have it, even
though you really want it?

Having an idea of what you want when it's all over will
help guide you through the dark and difficult parts of the
curve. It becomes the light at the end of the tunnel. It also
gives you something to be positive about and to hold on to,
when the rest of your life may seem crazy and chaotic.
Remember to bring this "ideal" image to mind frequently as
you continue your transition journey.

Knowing Your Fears
Lots of people making life changes discover parts of themselves they didn't know were there. Some of these are great

and others they'd rather have kept hidden. What they also
find is that when they try to ignore the parts they don't like,
those parts disappear for a little while only to return later,
bigger than ever. Fears can come in many forms; knowing
what yours are and how they appear to you really helps to
ease the discomforts of Stage Three of the transition curve.

Here are a few of the common fears others have admitted
to us:

— fear of failure
— fear of success
— fear of intimacy
— fear of dying
— fear of the unknown
— fear of the dark
— fear of losing control
— fear of losing
— fear of making a fool of myself
— fear of being different
— fear of being abandoned
— fear of loneliness
— fear of responsibility
— fear of commitment
— (add more of your own)...

Some fear-based questions which often come up:

— can I keep control?
— will I ever trust enough to love again?
— am I really a violent person?
— am I going insane?
— am I lovable?
— will people respect me?
— will I ever be "normal" again?
— if there really were a God, how could this happen?

Use your note book to take a look at your own fears:

1. Under the heading "My Favorite Fears," write down the things you're most afraid of in yourself and those closest to you.

2. Look over each one and see if you can remember an event or message that could be the source of the fear. Closing your eyes may help you remember.

3. When you look back at your earlier transition experiences, can you see how these fears played themselves out?

4. Is there anything you can do to alleviate the fears?

Talking to someone about your fears, or drawing a simple picture of what a fear might look like if it had a "personality" may help. You'll also find that holding the attitude that fears are real and have a legitimate purpose can often take away some of their ability to immobilize you. A dear friend once told us, "Fear can be a wonderful servant but a lousy master."

One little note here: Knowing what your fears are doesn't make them go away, but it sure helps when you're down in the "pit" because they no longer have so much power to surprise you. They'll almost certainly still be trying to get your attention and trying to stop you from getting on with things. Being in touch with them, and knowing that others probably have the same or similar fears, can make you feel better — and make the whole transition lots easier to handle.

Making Light Of Your Fears

There are a number of things you can do to release some of your feelings of fear and anxiety. We'll discuss restructuring some of your thinking patterns in Chapters Fourteen and

Fifteen, and in Chapter Sixteen we'll explore the value of good nutrition and exercise.

Among the major tools that can help you deal with anxiety is a therapeutic procedure called *systematic desensitization,* which was developed by Temple University psychiatrist Joseph Wolpe. It is based on the idea that you *learned* to be anxious about something and you can *unlearn* it. With the help of a psychotherapist, this process of desensitization helps you to associate the fear and anxiety you may feel about a situation with a deep sense of relaxation. As you practice the procedure, you will learn to feel relaxed whenever the anxiety promoting beliefs pop into your head.

The foundation of systematic desensitization is *very deep full-body relaxation.* That's a procedure which can be of great value in itself in dealing with everyday stress and tension. Practiced regularly it can be more refreshing than a nap. Here's an abbreviated overview of how it works:

• Close your eyes. Imagine yourself in a very safe and relaxing place. Gradually working from the tips of your toes to the top of your head, first tighten, then relax, each of the muscle groups in your body (feet, legs, torso, arms, etc.). Feel the tension leaving your body and a wave of relaxation waving over you. Let your mind focus on (a) further releasing any tightness in your body, and (b) visualizing your "safe place."

• Repeat this for ten to fifteen minutes a day over the next few days until you are finding it easy and comfortable. As it comes easier, you'll be able to relax more fully and more quickly. You may enjoy it so much you'll want to keep on practicing!

If you were to undertake systematic desensitization for a specific fear, the therapist would ask you to develop a list — in order of intensity — of six or eight scenes related to your fear (e.g. from "thinking about giving a speech" to "standing in front of a highly critical audience"). Then you'd be asked — under the therapist's supervision — to visualize each of the scenes related to your fear while you're relaxed, swapping back and forth in your mind every few seconds between your fear scene and your safe place scene.

Practicing this procedure over a period of weeks can help you develop a sense of relaxation each time the fear arises. The power it has to promote anxiety will begin to reduce, and you'll be able to face the feared situation (job interview, date, speech, exam, visit with in-laws) much more comfortably.

This is a simplified overview of the procedure but it gives you the basic idea of systematic desensitization. If the idea appeals to you for dealing with particularly strong irrational fears in your own life, we suggest you discuss it with a qualified behavioral therapist.

Developing skills in acting assertively is another good way to overcome some of your fears. Every time you step out and ask for what you truly want, or take a risk in the face of a fear, you reaffirm or take back the control you have of your life, leaving your fears with little or no power over you. One of the finest books on assertiveness is *Your Perfect Right* by Robert E. Alberti and Michael L. Emmons.

Many people have written about their experiences of change in story form. Some examples of these are *Jonathon Livingston Seagull* by Richard Bach, *Lord of the Rings* by J.R.R. Tolkien, and *Watership Down* by Richard Adams. More references are listed in the Appendix at the end of this book, but we think these are particularly useful in helping to look at life changes as adventures in growth.

Finding other people who have been through a similar life experience also can help. They may be able to give you ideas on how you can expect to feel and what is likely to happen as you make the adjustment. Although your experience is unique, other people's stories can be of great support, especially at those times when you think you're the only one who has ever thought or felt anything similar to this!

We all have our own stories, and sometimes it helps to look at them using mythical characters and other symbolic images, such as dragons and wizards, seagulls and sailboats, mountains and forests. For some people, a major life change can open a door into a whole world of pictures and mental images they never realized were there. Others may find themselves writing lots of poetry. Such a creative expression of your feelings can be both exciting and frightening when it first happens, but it is quite common among people who find their world in chaos. "Sleeping" parts of the subconscious begin to wake up and artistic talents get expressed in many new and different ways.

Although no transition can be guaranteed to be fear free, some of the ideas we have provided in this chapter, and others throughout the the book, are designed to make the whole experience easier to come to terms with.

12

WHERE TO FIND SUPPORT

In our years of working with people going through sig-nigicant life changes, we've learned that one of the most important elements of a successful transition is the quality of their relationships: with themselves; with their friends, family, and other people; and with the things around them. We refer to this as a "support system," and it includes people, things, values and ideas, the environment, and anything else that gives you support in one way or another.

People Who Are There For You

People who are extroverted may have lots of others to turn to during times of change; more introverted folks may have just one or two really close friends or family members who support them. Whichever description fits you best, it's impor-tant to note that it's not the numbers of people you have around you but the quality of their caring and understanding.

Having and using a good quality support system can speed your adjustment and lessen the pain of change.

• The following exercise asks you to think of the people you have around you who are supporting you in one way or another. You may not always "like" them, but in some way they are there for you. You may have one or two key people who fit all of the categories listed, and you may have some empty spaces. These spaces provide you with an opportunity to develop some new relationships or to expand some that you have already.

> 1. Take a few moments now to complete your "support system profile," listing the names in your life change notebook.

> My Support System

A. *Mind Stretchers*

People who help me think in new ways. People who are knowledgeable, pointing out new facts and ideas that help me learn.

B. *Health Nuts*

People who encourage me to be healthy, and confront me when I'm not taking care of myself. People who make me aware of my body and those who keep me warm on cold winter nights.

C. *Bright Lights*

People who hear my silent questions about life. Those who help me to be true to myself, and grow wise through my own experience. People who guide me to new ways of seeing the world, and help me find my own courage. Those who simply love me for who I am.

D. Safe Places

People with whom I share my hopes and fears and with whom I can talk about being vulnerable and human. People I can laugh with, and cry with, and tell about the good things and the bad.

E. Others

Those who are part of my support system, but don't really fit any of the above groups. Professional counselors and those who can help me get hold of things I need.

2. Now take a moment to look over your list and, using a pen with a different color ink, list the names of anyone you would *like* to have as part of your support system but hasn't already been mentioned.

3. Are there any areas in which you know you need to find some people to help you make the most of your transition?

You are bound to feel closer to some people than to others, but just knowing who is there for you will make changes less threatening. You'll also find that as you go through a major life change many of the names on the list will change. There may be some people whom you will grow away from because they want to hold you back. It's a good idea at this time to identify any people you need to let go of because they really don't support you anymore.

Other Forms Of Support

People often tell us of special places they go that give them a lot of support — such as a beach, a park, or somewhere else in nature. Others have a room of their own, or a favorite place in the house where they feel safe and peaceful.

Cats, dogs, and other pets can be wonderful sources of support, as can stuffed animals, a favorite picture, or a piece of music. Anything that helps you feel peaceful inside and gets you in touch with the loving parts of yourself can be part of your support system.

Keeping a log or a journal of your thoughts, feelings, dreams and experiences is often very helpful, particularly during times of change. If you have a tendency to withdraw from others when you get confused or upset (a great many people do), it can decrease the "down time" if you write out your thoughts and feelings on a piece of paper. Otherwise the angry thoughts and hurt feelings that usually accompany a major change may stay inside and cause you to feel stressed and even more confused.

You may find it supportive to take time to focus inward through meditation and prayer. Many of our participants talk about getting in touch with their quiet inner voice and learning to trust their intuition, rather than relying completely on what is logical. Some people are aware of a spiritual guide or a "guardian angel" who helps them work through their problems. Although these are less concrete forms of support, they can be incredibly valuable, especially during periods of change.

The more you know about yourself and the way you normally react to change — and the more you know about who and what you have around you to give you support — the better you'll be prepared to make the most of any change.

• Now add the following headings to your support system list and write down things that support you that are not people.

F. Special Things

Things I like to do or have around me.
My furry friends and lucky charms.

G. Favorite Places

Places where I go to find some peace and quiet. Places that hold special meaning for me.

H. Silent Gifts

Beliefs and ideals that give me the support I need to continue on my journey

Then, looking over your whole support system, remind yourself of the stages of the transition curve and be thinking of which ones are the most difficult for you and where you will need the most support. Is there anyone you could get in touch with today who could help you at this stage of your transition?

Professional Helpers

Many people find that they can get excellent support from a professional therapist, psychologist, psychiatrist, pastoral counselor, certified marriage and family counselor, or social worker when they are working through a life change.

It's at times like this that you may find yourself dealing with old "issues" that don't seem to have anything to do with the particular change. For example, a divorce may trigger some old feelings about your relationship with your parents or a past lover.

Often while you're in "the pit," all of that unfinished business you've been sitting on for many years will try to get your attention. Professional counseling can be incredibly supportive in helping you sort out all the "stuff." A counselor will be able to work with you to separate the different pieces so it's less confusing. Since the relationship is more objective and less personal than those of friends and family, a counselor can provide you with a great deal of safety in sharing some of the more difficult emotions and sensitive thoughts that you may not want to reveal to even the closest of your friends.

A qualified professional can also guide you through the procedures we have mentioned for dealing with fears and anxieties, relationship problems, letting go, and other obstacles to your progress through the seven stages. Don't settle for a random pick from the Yellow Pages, however. Ask friends, your doctor and other professionals, a trusted clergyperson, a local mental health center or college psychology clinic for referrals. When you call, ask the therapist for a no-fee "get acquainted" session, and interview two or three before you select someone with whom to work. Ask about fees, approach, experience with your specific needs. Select a counselor as carefully as you would a physician.

13

SKILLS WHICH
WILL BE HELPFUL

We've talked a lot about the value of knowing yourself and the way you handle changes. Valuable, too, are skills that will help you cope with the many demands and pressures of any transition. Since most of us nowadays are usually "in transition," it helps to think of these as "life skills," not techniques to be taken out and used just during the tougher times of a transition.

A lot of the ideas and suggestions in this chapter come from people we have worked with over the years; others grow out of our work in stress management and health promotion programs. We don't expect that anyone will find *all* of these suggestions to be useful, but we think that each of you will find some that are really helpful.

We'll be asking you to think about four types of skills and then to draw some conclusions about what you need to do to strengthen your own skill collection. After we describe these four groups of skills, we'll ask you to fill in a brief questionnaire so you can find out how you're doing and what more you can do to help yourself with your transition.

We've called the first set *Avoidance Skills*. They are needed to remove unnecessary sources of stress, and to help you avoid taking on any more unnecessary pressures as you go through the most challenging stages of the transition. These skills include such things as knowing your strengths and weaknesses and being able to manage your time.

Then we have *Coping Skills*. You'll need these to deal with unavoidable pressures and challenges. This set is made up of interpersonal or social skills, such as assertiveness, working with conflict, and being able to solve problems.

Next are *Preparation Skills*. They help you focus on the future, plan for what you think will happen and get ready for it. They'll also help you decide what kind of future you want and how to take steps to create it.

We call the fourth set *Self-Management Skills*. These, like many of the others, are important at all times. Transitions are often very stressful, and can sometimes cause health problems if you don't look after yourself. The old saying that "an ounce of prevention is better than a pound of cure" makes very good sense. People should practice good self-management skills regularly; it may be too late to begin practicing them after a long period of stress. The value of these skills builds over time. In Chapter Sixteen, we take a more detailed look at how to stay healthy during difficult times.

As you complete the following questionnaire, you'll find that you already have some of the skills in each of the four areas. This isn't a complete list of skills; you can add your own ideas in each area. You may also find that some of those we have included in one area would fit better for you in a different area. Please rearrange the questionnaire in any way that makes it useful for you. If you prefer, use your notebook to identify the areas in which you need to improve.

TRANSITION SKILLS QUESTIONNAIRE

I. Avoidance Skills

	DOING FINE	NEED IMPROVEMENT
1. I say "no" to new involvements or responsibilities.	____	____
2. I am clear about my priorities and I manage my time well.	____	____
3. I put off or ignore low priority activities.	____	____
4. I ask for advice, challenge and/or guidance from others.	____	____
5. I think about my situation and keep it in perspective.	____	____
6. I draw on what has helped me in previous transitions.	____	____
7. I avoid repeating mistakes I made during other transitions.	____	____

8. I review my various
   commitments and rela-
   tionships periodically,   _____   _____
   and withdraw from
   those that are no
   longer good for me.

9.   _____   _____

10.   _____   _____

Now take a moment to make some notes to yourself about what you need to do to *avoid* the unnecessary problems and pressures of your transition.

II. Coping Skills

	DOING FINE	*NEED IMPROVEMENT*
1. I meet the challenges of my transitions head on.	_____	_____
2. I know what I want most of the time.	_____	_____
3. I take the initiative in new situations to get what I want.	_____	_____

4. I ask for support,
   direct assistance,
   expertise and/or feed-   _____   _____
   back from others.

5. I take quiet time
   for myself for prayer,
   meditation, visuali-   _____   _____
   zation.

6. I take breaks for
   relaxation and/or   _____   _____
   diversion.

7. I use the self-fulfilling
   prophecy and ask for   _____   _____
   what I want.

8. I am assertive about
   my wants and needs.   _____   _____

9. I explore the options
   and the possibilities   _____   _____
   in my present situation.

10. I consider the specific
    details and requirements   _____   _____
    in my present situation.

11. I consider my feelings
    and values when I make   _____   _____
    decisions.

12. I use my skills of rational analysis before making decisions.   _____   _____

13. I avoid jumping to conclusions, and make sure I keep things open-ended.   _____   _____

14. I avoid procrastinating and act decisively.   _____   _____

15. I create small successes and set *very* short-term goals.   _____   _____

16. I separate what is real from what is imagined.   _____   _____

17. I talk to others who have been in my situation.   _____   _____

18. I know the difference between what I can control and what I can't control.   _____   _____

19.   _____   _____

20.   _____   _____

Take a moment to make some notes to yourself about how well you are *coping* with the unavoidable problems and pressures of your transition.

III. Preparation Skills

	DOING FINE	NEEDS IMPROVEMENT
1. I have a clear sense of my true life purpose.	_____	_____
2. I think about "possible futures" and prepare for them.	_____	_____
3. I create visions of the future I want and take steps to create it.	_____	_____
4. I live my life with truth and integrity.	_____	_____
5. I set goals and objectives for myself.	_____	_____
6. I experiment with new ways to handle recurring situations.	_____	_____
7. I talk to others about the future I expect and/or want.	_____	_____
8. I have personal groundrules to guide my actions.	_____	_____
9. I create "safe places" where I go to be taken care of.	_____	_____

10. I stay away from negative,
    angry, depressed people   _____   _____
    as much as I can.

11.   _____   _____

12.   _____   _____

Now take a moment to make some notes to yourself about
how well you *prepare* for the problems and pressures you may
come across as the transition continues to unfold.

IV. Self-Management Skills

	Doing *Fine*	*Need* *Improvement*
1. I have a good quality exercise program.	_____	_____
2. I relax and meditate regularly.	_____	_____
3. I eat a balanced diet, — low in fat, salt, sugar and added chemicals — that provides me with plenty of vitamins, minerals and fiber.	_____	_____
4. I get enough restful sleep.	_____	_____

5. I keep to my recom-
   mended weight.   _____   _____

6. I do not smoke.   _____   _____

7. I use alcohol in
   moderation, if at all.   _____   _____

8. I always wear seat
   belts.   _____   _____

9. I drive defensively
   and carefully.   _____   _____

10. My self-talk is
    positive and caring.   _____   _____

11. My general outlook is
    positive and optimistic.   _____   _____

12. I have plenty of
    supportive relationships.   _____   _____

13. I do not count on
    drugs to get me through   _____   _____
    the tough parts of life.

14.   _____   _____

15.   _____   _____

Make some notes to yourself about continuing with those
self-management skills that keep you healthy and optimistic
about the future.

As you look over your answers, develop a plan that strengthens and adds to your collection of transition skills, by completing the following:

A. In each area what are three (or more) of your strongest skills?

I. Avoidance

II. Coping

III. Preparation

IV. Self-Management

B. For each of the areas write down what skills you think you most need to *begin* doing or do *more frequently* to make your transition easier.

I. Avoidance

II. Coping

III. Preparation

IV. Self-Management

C. In each area write down what you think you most need to *stop* doing or do *less frequently* to help you with this transition.

I. Avoidance

II. Coping

III. Preparation

IV. Self-Management

D. Looking back at B and C, take one area you would like to improve and write it down as a first project. For example, under *Self-Management* you may have identified Number 1, "I have a good quality exercise program" as something you need to improve. Think about what you can do to improve your exercise habits, such as beginning a walking program.

E. What are the first few steps you will take to get started on this project? (Buying a pair of good quality walking shoes is an example.)

F. Think about the ways other people can make sure you're successful in this project. Write down the names of anyone who can provide you with support, and note how they can be helpful.

G. Make a note of how you will know when you have been successful. What are some specific ways you'll measure your success? (For example, "My pulse rate is lowered to 65 beats per minute.")

As you can see, we are suggesting a one-step-at-a-time approach to building skills. We've found that the people who have been most successful at strengthening their transition skills are the ones who do it in this way. Those people who try to do it all at once — and both of us have done that more times than we'd like to admit — often stay with the "new" only a short while. We start with great enthusiasm, then gradually drift back to "normal." Remember, when you take on a new skill you'll probably go through a mini-transition to make it part of your life.

WHY BELIEFS ARE SO IMPORTANT

In this chapter we'll cover the importance of your beliefs, assumptions, values, and expectations, and the role they play in your life, especially during times of change. In a book which deals specifically with this area, known as "cognitive psychology," these topics would be separated more distinctly, but for now we'll consider them all together.

Where Do They Come From?

According to most research on human development, basic beliefs, assumptions and values are pretty much in place by the time a person reaches ten to twelve years of age. The experiences you had early in your life, and the repeated messages you heard from your parents and teachers in these first few years, have formed the basis of your outlook on life and your beliefs. These then influence how you see the world

and lead you to have certain ideas about "changes" — which
are good changes and which are bad. The beliefs that you hold
have an important influence on how you handle life changes.

Let's spend a little longer taking a look at this whole area
of beliefs. A participant in a recent workshop suggested that
"to believe in" is almost the same as "to be alive in" and that
beliefs form the framework for the experience of life. That is,
our beliefs at some level are always influencing what we
experience. If we believe that change is to be avoided because
it "rocks the boat" and others won't like us for doing that, then
we'll probably avoid making changes. Sometimes we stay in
a situation even though it is uncomfortable because we fear
the consequences of making a change.

  • *Jim had been married for seventeen years and had
  been unhappy for the last ten. In the early days he had
  tried a number of things to make it better — couples
  counseling, second honeymoons and the like. Things did
  not improve — yet still he stayed. Finally, after he and
  his wife had been living separate lives under the same
  roof for six years, he left the marriage. When somebody
  asked him why he stayed those ten years, even though he
  knew it wasn't working, he remembered that as a child
  when people got divorced they became the talk of the town
  and were disapproved of by the community. He didn't
  want the same thing happening to him.*

  *Although society's view of divorce has changed consid-
  erably since Jim was a boy, somewhere outside his conscious awareness he still believed that he would be
  disapproved of and become the subject of local gossip.
  When he brought this belief to the surface, he recognized
  how strong the message had been and how it had been
  the main reason for staying in his unhappy marriage all
  those years.*

How Will I Recognize Them?

We all have beliefs that are hard at work, causing us to see the world and react to changes in certain ways. Depending on those early messages, you will hold certain attitudes and outlooks about who you are and what you can and cannot do. It is important, especially during times of change, to bring some of your old beliefs to the surface, and to decide if they are still good for you. It's a little like clearing out the attic and finding things that should have been thrown out years ago, along with other things that are in perfect condition but need a little dusting off.

To take this idea a little further, you will need your journal. Thinking back to your childhood, write down some of the messages you remember being repeated over and over by your parents or other key adults in those early years — messages such as: "Don't cross the road without mommy"; "Don't take sweets from strangers because you can't trust them"; "Do as you're told"; "Do your best"; "You're not old enough yet."

We all heard messages like these when we were children. They were probably good for us most of the time — to ensure our safety and well-being. The more often they were repeated, however, the more they hypnotized us. As a result many of us are holding onto beliefs that have long outlived their usefulness, and yet still are "grinding away" beyond our conscious awareness.

"Do as you're told" can later get interpreted as "don't use your own initiative, wait until someone tells you what to do." "Don't take sweets from strangers ..." maybe interpreted as "don't accept compliments because you can't always trust the person who gives them to you, and they may expect something in return."

> • *A young research worker did a super job in meeting the very short deadline his boss had set. When the boss told him what an excellent job he had done, the research worker said he didn't pay any attention to the compliment because he thought the boss would only give him an even shorter deadline next time.*

We've found lots of cases where people can't even hear positive feedback about who they are and what they've done because they believe they can't trust the motivation of the person giving it to them.

As a further example, we often hear people of retirement age report sadly during our workshops that they never did get "old enough" to do what they really wanted during their careers. They find that an important message they heard when they were children has been playing itself out all those years, and had become such a deep-rooted belief that they never really lived.

Have a look at the messages you noted in your journal and see how they may be influencing some of the choices you are making today. Then put a check mark against those you want to keep and a question mark against those you think may no longer be of value.

Uncovering some of these "old tapes" will help you find some of the key factors that control or limit your opportunities to make the most of life changes. They may even be causing you to feel a lot more pain and fear than necessary!

What Else Do Beliefs Do?

Beliefs have a number of other characteristics that can support or defeat us during times of change and transition.

Beliefs tend to be *self-fulfilling.* If you believe a certain thing is going to happen, then the chances are much better that it will.

• *After years of believing that she was "just" a secretary, Sandra got fed up with being treated like a second-class citizen in her office. When she realized that she was helping to make it so by believing her role was unimportant, she decided to look at things differently. She soon recognized and believed that the secretarial role really was important to the success of her department and suggested she should attend meetings and be a key player in some of the office decisions. From the moment she began to think differently, Sandra said her whole view of her job changed. Significantly, so too did people's attitudes toward her.*

This example shows how the self-fulfilling prophecy can work for you or against you, and suggests that the more clearly you choose what you want to believe, the more likely you'll get what you want. If people don't make conscious choices about their beliefs and outlooks, they will probably end up reacting to the world around them, feeling as though they are the victims of other people or the circumstances surrounding them.

Beliefs tend to be *self-reinforcing*. This means that the more they come true, the more strongly we believe them. For example, if you believe you have nothing of value to say, or that people won't understand, then you probably won't say very much. Then, when you do get around to saying something and others don't pay much attention, you'll probably believe even more strongly that you don't have anything important to say.

On the other hand if you believe that you can have what you want in life, then even when you come across road blocks, you will see them as challenges to be overcome. After successfully dealing with the challenges, you will believe even more strongly that you can have what you want in life.

Beliefs tend to be *self-limiting*. As a result of repeated messages heard as children, many of the beliefs people hold about themselves hold them back. Early "be careful" messages can lead to avoiding risks later that may be needed to get what is wanted or needed.

Also, anytime you say "I can't..." or "I don't have time to..." you are programming yourself to believe that you are *incapable*. You will do better and have more control over your own destiny if you replace "I can't" with "I won't," and "I don't have time" with "I won't make time." These replacements send the message that you are making choices, whereas the "I can't" messages suggest that you are powerless to change things.

In a public lecture, teacher of creativity Robert Fritz told of a study in which children carried tape recorders to find out what kind of messages they received from their parents and teachers. When the tapes were analyzed, about 90 percent of the messages were statements of a limiting nature, such as "No, that's wrong;" "You should do it this way;" "Be quiet;" and so on. Our first reaction was that his findings must be exaggerated. But since then we have listened to parents with their children — even in our own families — and have to report that in some cases it's even more than 90 percent.

In a lecture on business innovation, social philosopher George Ainsworth-Land referred to a study of the potential for innovation among different age groups. At age five, he reported, 98 percent of those tested were judged to have high potential for innovation; at age ten, the number had dropped to 32 percent; at age fifteen it was down to 12 percent; and by age thirty, only 2 percent were judged to have high potential to be innovative. At age sixty, the figure had risen to 7 percent and was climbing. People over age sixty were found to pick up new and innovative ideas faster than any other age group!

This could mean that as we become educated in the ways of our society, we become less likely to "test" and step outside the accepted ways of believing and behaving. After retirement, we feel free to become who we *really* are because there's no-one "older and bigger" than us and we no longer have "bosses." Up to a point, there has to be order in society, but when it limits the opportunity for people to grow, it is time to look at whether such beliefs have outlived their usefulness.

Beliefs *resist change* and attempt to *influence others* to share the same view of life. As your beliefs receive reinforcement over the years and become more firmly entrenched, it becomes more difficult to change them. You will behave in ways which keep your outlook the way it has always been, and which try to convince others that your point of view is the "right" one. In order to develop new beliefs, and to remain open to other ideas, you may have to work hard to overcome this normal tendency. Think about it, next time you're trying to get someone to change.

- *Linda, a friend of ours, recently decided to leave her job in search of more excitement in her life. After a few months, she gave up and took a job very similar to the one she had just left, saying that she needed the security of the familiar. Whenever people reminded her about her earlier decision to seek something new, she quickly gave them a number of reasons why it had been a silly idea.*

  On some level, Linda didn't want to let go of her old beliefs, and tried to convince others that her present viewpoint was absolutely the only one possible. When Linda was able to let go of the beliefs that caused her to renege on her wish for more adventure in her life, she grew very excited and knew she could do what she really wanted. Today, Linda has her own small business and, although it is not as secure as "a real job," she wouldn't want it any other way.

Staying awake to the deep messages that may be controlling you can be very rewarding, especially during times of change when they tend to pop to the surface. It is much easier to recognize and get rid of old, unwanted beliefs when you are in transition than at any other time.

15

HOW TO KEEP
A POSITIVE ATTITUDE

In the last chapter, we described what beliefs are, where they come from and how they work. We can now look more specifically at those that will help you keep a positive attitude during times of change. We'll also identify those that can get in your way.

Beliefs That Help/Beliefs That Get In The Way
 • Once more using your journal or notebook, list under the heading "Beliefs That Help in Making Changes" all the beliefs you have ever heard that support change — such as that change leads to growth; change provides challenging opportunities; change is natural and healthy; change is good for you.
 • Put a check mark beside any of the beliefs which you think may be influencing *you* positively or negatively.

• Next, answer these questions about each "helpful" belief:

How would it help me?

Would not believing it hold me back?

What would happen if I *really* believed it?

• Now, repeat them to yourself several times. By doing this, you can shift your attitude toward changes and you may find it easier to deal with them than before.

• Make another list, under the heading "Beliefs That Get In the Way," of all the beliefs you have ever heard that get in the way of making changes — for example; if it's good it will last forever; people who change are basically unhappy; if it ain't broke, don't fix it.

• Put a check mark beside any of the beliefs which *you* think may be influencing you positively or negatively.

• See if you can remember where you first heard each of these "in the way" beliefs, and decide if you want to believe them any more by answering these questions:

Does it help me?

Does it stop me getting what I really want?

What will happen if I let go of this belief?

• If you no longer feel you need a particular belief — put a heavy line through it.

It is always important to recognize that change brings both positives and negatives. Those who only see the positive side often find it difficult to come to terms with the more difficult parts of the transition process. Those who only see the negative side will miss some positive opportunities that the transition offers, and may put lots of energy into resisting making changes altogether. We urge you to keep a balanced outlook, notice both the up-side and the down-side of any change, and always look for opportunities to grow.

Your Beliefs About Yourself

The beliefs you hold about yourself also can help you to face changes positively and with a spirit of adventure, or they can lead you to fear change and see only the potential for loss and pain. As with the more general beliefs discussed in the last section, it is important to explore your beliefs about yourself—those that support you in life and those that inhibit you. If this is overlooked, your body/mind system's natural tendency to protect itself from changes will make your transition more difficult.

As you go through a major transition, you'll find that some days you feel good about yourself and other days you may not like yourself as much. These shifts in your self-esteem are a natural part of the adjustment process. We have found that those people who hold mostly positive beliefs about themselves are able to move through the uncomfortable parts of the life change curve with less difficulty than those who hold lots of negative and limiting beliefs about themselves.

Of course, all of us have some of each, but during times of change when there is a lot of uncertainty around, your self-limiting beliefs will try very hard to get your attention. Knowing what they are and replacing them with beliefs that support you can be very helpful.

Self-Limiting Beliefs: These are some of the most common self-limiting beliefs:

I can't have what I want.	I am powerless.
Others know what's best for me.	I'm not ready yet.
No one understands me.	If they really knew me...
I'm not experienced enough.	I don't have control.

I don't deserve real success.	Fate will decide.
I always...	I never...

How many of these are you aware of having said to yourself from time to time? Add any other self-limiting beliefs you hold about yourself that are not listed above.

Self-Supporting Beliefs: Let's look at the other side of the equation, and identify some of the self-supporting beliefs you already have working for you. These beliefs will lead you to what you want in life and help you remain strong during times of change.

Some common self-supporting beliefs:

I can have what I want.	I can have it all.
I know what to do.	Life is an adventure.
I can trust others.	People will help me.
I can trust my hunches.	I have the skills I need.

Once more, write down those that are true for you and add some more of your own. If this doesn't come easy, make up some new beliefs that you'd like to have.

Changing Unwanted Beliefs

To help you keep a positive attitude during times of transition you can change any beliefs that are getting in your way. One way to do this is by creating affirmations.

Follow this easy process:

- Identify a belief you don't want anymore and write it

down. For example, "I can't control the situation" or "I always get impatient."

• Now turn it into a positive statement that supports you — "I am in control and can have what I want" or "I am patient and calm."

Be careful to avoid writing "I should" or "I will" — this puts it into the future and the "old belief" continues to operate.

• Write your *new* belief on a piece of paper that you can carry with you, and repeat it as often as possible to yourself during the next few weeks.

Replacing old, unwanted beliefs can be very straightforward — though it may take a while — once you have discovered which ones no longer work for you. By repeating the affirmation over and over to yourself, you will gradually reprogram your mind and start getting different results. If you are hesitant about this process, *act as if it works* for a few weeks and see what happens.

We have encouraged you to use affirmations to help you move through the stages of the transition curve more speedily. But even with their help, there still will be times when you'll notice that one of your old, self-limiting beliefs is working against you.

Whenever you find this is happening, reduce the power of the old belief and reinforce the new one by first recognizing that the old one is trying to get your attention and then *choosing* the new one instead. As an example, if you are aware that you are becoming impatient, you should accept that this is happening and remind yourself that you are choosing to remain calm. After a few times, the new belief will begin to have more influence than the old one, especially in reference to situations that made you impatient in the past.

Beliefs About Personal Value

It is important to hold positive attitudes toward yourself, other people, and about life in general — even though on darker days you may find yourself leaning quite the opposite direction. Your attitudes toward yourself will strongly influence how you deal with any transition. The more you believe in yourself and believe the change will have a positive outcome, the more likely you are to get positive results.

This last activity is designed to help you stay positive throughout the transition. By finishing the following sentences in your notebook, you will find out what you believe to be of value about yourself. These are the qualities that help to make you a unique human being, and they are important to hold on to when self-doubt knocks at your door.

> I make a difference by...
>
> My most special gifts are...
>
> I am grateful for my ...
>
> I truly enjoy the way I...
>
> My life is richer because I...
>
> I am excited by how I...
>
> My relationships give me...
>
> What I value most about myself is...

Whenever you find that you're slipping into being negative you can use these statements to put a smile back on your face. Sometimes, it is good idea to have a friend go over your responses with you, helping you rediscover how great you really are. It's easy to forget how good life is when we're groping around in the dark. Keep this list close at hand and take a look at it whenever you begin to doubt yourself; it can really help you feel positive again.

16

HOW TO STAY HEALTHY AND MANAGE STRESS

A time of change often leads us to giving up good habits, over-indulging in bad ones, and becoming generally more vulnerable to health risks. If you're feeling high levels of stress as you make your transition, you will probably find the next three points — and all the rest of the information in this chapter — very helpful.

First, stress is a major risk to health. *Second,* during times of change most people do a *poorer* job of taking care of themselves than they do during more stable periods. *Third,* in the general population, daily lifestyle choices make up well over half of the risks to health.

What Exactly Is Stress?

When you are under stress, your body makes internal adjustments to cope with everything — and this triggers what is known as "the fight or flight response." This is a biological response that evolved to help our earliest ancestors cope with the stressors of the day — usually threats to survival, like fighting off a saber-tooth tiger! Today, the stressors that come with divorce, being fired, and so on, don't normally threaten people's physical survival, but our bodies haven't kept pace with civilization, and they still respond to stressors in the same way as they did thousands of years ago — by getting ready for quick action.

The problem arises when we don't develop healthy and appropriately contemporary responses to stressors. It's certainly not a good idea to punch the boss or run through the house screaming in response to transition stress. But if you develop good stress management habits — balanced nutrition, plenty of exercise, regular relaxation, solid interpersonal relationships — you'll be equipped to handle the tough times without illness or other major problems.

How Much Is Stress Costing You?

Carrying around too much strain (fight or flight preparedness) for any length of time increases your risk of becoming ill. The following list of conditions will give you an indication of how much stress is costing you. Rate yourself from 1 to 5, depending on how frequently each item has been true for you during the past two or three weeks:

1 = Rarely or never

2 = Occasionally

3 = Sometimes

4 = Frequently

5 = Always

_____ 1. Eat too much.

_____ 2. Drink too much alcohol.

_____ 3. Smoke more than usual.

_____ 4. Feel tense, uptight, fidgety, nervous.

_____ 5. Feel depressed or remorseful.

_____ 6. Like myself less.

_____ 7. Have difficulty going to sleep or staying asleep.

_____ 8. Feel restless and unable to concentrate.

_____ 9. Have decreased interest in sex.

_____ 10. Have increased interest in sex.

_____ 11. Have loss of appetite.

_____ 12. Feel tired, low energy, excessive fatigue.

_____ 13. Feel irritable.

_____ 14. Think about suicide.

_____ 15. Become less communicative.

_____ 16. Feel disoriented or overwhelmed.

_____ 17. Have difficulty getting up in the morning.

_____ 18. Have headaches.

_____ 19. Have upset stomach or intestinal problems.

_____ 20. Have sweaty and/or trembling hands.

_____ 21. Have shortness of breath — sighing.

_____ 22. Let things slide.

_____ 23. Show misdirected anger.

_____ 24. Feel "unhealthy."

_____ 25. Feel weak.

_____ 26. Feel dizzy or lightheaded.

— TOTAL STRAIN SCORE

Each item on this strain questionnaire may arise as a result of over-taxing the endocrine system, especially the thyroid and adrenal glands, through a prolonged, continuous triggering of the fight or flight response.

After collecting total scores for several years from a wide variety of people, we've found that a total score of 50 or greater may represent a risk to your health — especially if you feel you expect a score at least this high over a long period. If your score is above 69, you are in the top 10 percent of the nearly 3,000 scores we have collected, and you need to think seriously about bringing it down, since higher scores suggest more extensive depletion of health reserves. We'll talk about how you can do that in a moment.

You probably recognize a few specific conditions above as being especially true for you from time to time. These are your "red flags." As a first step in good transition management, you need to become sensitive to when you get these early warning signals. Their presence indicates that your strain level is getting too high and that you need to get rid of some of the avoidable sources of stress, cope with the unavoidable ones better, and build up your health reserves so you can better withstand the pressure.

Unfortunately, when most of us are going through major transitions, we make our problems worse by giving up our best defenses. For example, have you ever withdrawn from your friends during the most difficult stages of a change? After you've passed through these stages do you resurface and begin calling friends, telling them what a rough period you've just been through? It's as if you feel you must handle it yourself, and not bother others, even when you know that drawing on supportive relationships is one of the most important transition management techniques.

Ways To Protect Your Health

There are three excellent ways you can reduce your strain score if it is higher than is good for you: 1) vigorous regular exercise, 2) frequent relaxation practices, and 3) a well-balanced diet.

Physical Exercise. Whenever you are experiencing the difficult parts of making an adjustment, your body responds with the stress response, which — as mentioned earlier — quite literally prepares you to get into a fight or to run away.

Exercise routines such as jogging, brisk walking, swimming, bicycling, and so on, are all acceptable forms of "flight"; while other sports like baseball, racquetball, tennis and football are popular forms of "fight." If you are willing to put in a minimum of three twenty-minute sessions per week participating in one of these forms of exercise, your body will burn up much of the fight or flight energy, you'll build your capacity to handle stress, ... and you'll be in better shape, too! (Adams, 1989; Cooper, 1983).

Regular Relaxation. Regular relaxation practices — such as meditation, prayer, sitting in the garden, and so on — are a form of (mental) flight. Whenever you allow yourself to relax completely, your brain will stop sending out fight or flight messages, and begin sending relaxation messages to all of the parts of your body. So, when you find that you are in the darker parts of the transition process, remember to relax for several minutes at least once a day. Just taking three or four long deep breaths from time to time really helps, but it's most effective to practice a deeper, full-body relaxation technique (Benson, 1975).

Eating Right. Many folks allow wise eating habits to be "put on the shelf" during periods of change, and eat foods high in fat, sugar, salt and added chemicals (that is, highly refined or "junk" foods). At the same time, many will drink or smoke more than usual, perhaps to get some relief or to lessen the strain feelings. Unfortunately, these behaviors add more risk factors to those already created by the transition, and keep the body from getting the nutrients it needs to fight stress.

The B and C vitamins are burned up very rapidly during periods of high stress. Alcohol, caffeine, tobacco and sugar may also take those vitamins away from their main purpose of keeping us healthy and functioning in balance — so the short-term "high" from eating, drinking or breathing these substances sets up long term health risks. Most of the B and C vitamins are found in fruits, vegetables, grains and nuts — foods that most people don't eat enough of, even in the best of times.

During the pressures of major changes, if you rely *only* on the convenience of fast foods like beer, burgers and fries, and bars of chocolate, you may find yourself in trouble. Most of us eat far too much salt, fat and sugar during our most stable periods, and then take in even greater amounts when experiencing long-term stress. In the final chapter, we have put together some menu suggestions you can use as guidelines for a healthy, more balanced diet as you continue to adjust to your change. Of course, the occasional beer or ice cream won't harm you, but overdoing it will.

Staying Healthy

Investigations of the most frequent major illnesses carried out regularly by the Centers for Disease Control in Atlanta, and the National Center for Health Statistics in Washington, D.C., suggest that about 18 percent of the risks to our health are biological (inherited from our parents or as a result of earlier illnesses or injuries); about 18 percent are environmental (air and water quality for example); and about 10 percent are due to health care services (inaccurate diagnoses, drug interactions and side effects).

This leaves about 54 percent of the risk factors under our everyday control, in a category called "lifestyle choices." Put another way, we can avoid more than half the risks to our health by making careful daily choices. So, if you want to stay healthy at times of transition — and beyond — the best thing to do is to control the controllables.

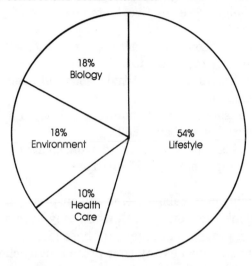

Risk Factors That Affect Health

The following list shows most of the risk factors you can control in the lifestyle category, including exercise, relaxation and nutrition. As you look over the list, keep track of how many you are currently practicing.

- Balanced diet (the average person consumes far too much sugar, fats, protein, salt, chemicals, white flour and caffeine; and needs many more fruits, vegetables, nuts and grains).
- Alcohol (no more than two alcoholic drinks per day on average). Tobacco (avoid tobacco completely).
- Drug use (avoid all "recreational" drugs and minimize use of prescription drugs).
- Amount of rest (average person needs 7 – 8 hours of sleep per day).
- Regular relaxation.

- Exercise (vigorously, at least three times a week for twenty to thirty minutes; stretching and recreational exercises are also good stress relievers).
- Body weight (within five to ten pounds of your ideal weight).
- Psychological outlook (positive, optimistic, self-aware).
- High-quality relationships.
- Driving habits (speed, attitude, seat belt use).
- Low strain scores.
- Blood pressure (regular monitoring, below 130/90).
- Cholesterol level (below 200).
- Minimizing type A behavior (driven, easily irritated, frequently impatient, cynical mistrust).

Few, if any of the above items will surprise you. Yet a lot of people don't come out so well when they have a good look at their own practices in regard to these factors. Take a few moments to see how healthy your present daily choices are.

The more items on this list you practice regularly, the better your everyday health is likely to be, and the longer you are likely to live. Are there some things you need to stop doing or cut down on? Are there some things you need to start doing or do more of? Pick one thing and start today.

17

WHY HAVING A PURPOSE HELPS

Most of us from time to time get a feeling of being "all together" and really feeling on top of the world, but it often isn't very long before something comes along and knocks us off center. In this chapter we'll talk about how you can stay "up" longer, and shorten the "down" times.

Let's assume that all of us are made up of three interconnected systems: the mind and our thoughts; the body and our behaviors; and the emotions and our feelings. That is, we think, we act, and we feel. Whenever anyone experiences a major life change, each of these parts will be affected in one way or another.

For example, if you are in the middle of a divorce, you may find that you have trouble "thinking straight" and that concentration is difficult. Also you may not want to do as much physically as usual, feeling instead as though you are "dragging yourself around." You may feel angry or sad one minute, and happy the next, all without warning. Whatever you find your experience to be, it is likely that a major change will affect you on all three levels.

Life Without Purpose

Without a clear sense of personal purpose, people are more at the mercy of the outside world. That means that as long as things are moving along comfortably, they will have the experience of being "all together." But, as soon as changes come along, the balance among the mind, body and emotions gets disturbed, and they are likely to feel as if they have been knocked off center, as shown in the diagram below. In many ways, it is like being on a ship without a rudder in the middle of a storm — feeling out of control.

The large amount of time and energy spent just surviving each successive change experience could otherwise be used to make the most of the new learning that is always there.

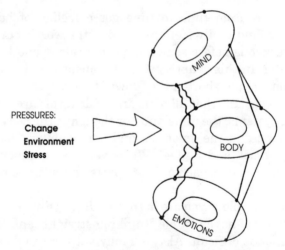

When people are knocked off balance they often experience higher levels of stress and, as noted in Chapter Sixteen, they may get sick more often. Purpose not only helps people stay healthy and clear about how they can make a difference, it can also make passage through the transition experience a great deal easier. If you don't have a sense of purpose in your life, Stage Three is likely to be much more traumatic, especially if the change is one which is high in novelty.

The Power Of Purpose

One of the best things you can do for yourself, to make sure that you have control over how you deal with changes, is to have a clear sense of personal purpose. When you know what you want from life, you will create a central core, like a spine that will keep the three parts in balance. You will *choose* how to think, feel and act rather than just reacting to one thing after another.

This also helps reduce the impact of the outside world and allows you to keep your energy focused in the direction you have *chosen* for yourself. Without a sense of purpose, the environment has a tremendous amount of power over what you experience. With a core purpose, the outside forces remain, and continue to have an impact, but their power is greatly reduced — (see the diagram below.)

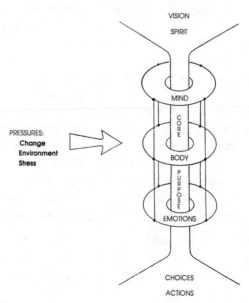

Purpose is the deeper meaning people give to life, work and relationships. It is the "spiritual backbone" and it helps people to value and to find the benefits in all of life's experiences. In the middle of a major transition — especially during Stage Three — a clear sense of purpose acts as a guiding light through the dark days. It helps show the reason for and the value of the changes, although it may not take away the pain.

Being clear about your own life's purpose won't take away the experiences we've described throughout the transition process. You will still find yourself reacting on all three levels. But you will discover that with a clear purpose, even during the most painful moments of a transition you'll actually experience a sense of excitement. And you'll find that you get "back on track" more quickly after each of these difficult moments.

Purpose And Spirit

For a lot of people the spiritual aspect of their lives is the hardest to understand because it can't really be measured and it's hard to see. It helps to remember how you've felt when you were really inspired, or to recall a sense of team spirit.

As shown in our second diagram above, we see spirit as a special source of energy, always available to us but much clearer when we are in touch with a higher sense of purpose.

Sometimes people who have been through a major life change describe experiences which got them in touch with other parts of themselves that they didn't know were there. Their descriptions range from feeling that someone was with them, to seeing lights (auras) around people, to remembering past lives and experiencing a feeling of being reborn.

- *Most people would describe Art as being very logical and down to earth, and so would he. In the middle of a very stressful period when he was changing jobs and trying to come to terms with the death of his seventeen-year-old son, he said he was lying in bed one night and suddenly found that he was looking down at himself. He moved freely around the room and up through the ceiling and the roof of the house, before he felt scared and rushed back to his physical body. For a while he didn't talk about it because he was afraid of being thought of as crazy. When he did, however, Art found that he had had an "out of body experience." What's more, not only have others experienced it, there even are books on the subject.*

This and similar experiences are not particularly uncommon during a major change that's very high in novelty. It seems that in the chaos and the stress, people sometimes lose their attachment to believing that they are confined to the physical world and open themselves to amazing new spiritual experiences. The illustration below suggests that at the time when we are at our lowest on the life change curve, we may feel most elated and have the greatest insights on a spiritual curve. In fact, it is often a major life change that leads people to identify or rediscover the true purpose of their lives.

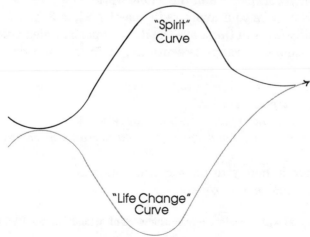

Developing A Purpose Statement*

The following steps are designed to help you get a clearer sense of your life purpose. They build a framework you can use to find out a little more about what you want to do with your life.

1. Looking back over your notes, identify three qualities or characteristics about yourself that are extremely important to you and write them down. For example, "My three most important qualities are my sense of humor, my creativity, and my caring for people."

2. Now think about how you usually express these qualities. For example, "I most often express these qualities in my talking, writing, supervising people, or creating fun projects."

3. How can you use your answers to questions 1 and 2 to give more meaning to your life? For example, "I encourage people to be positive, I want to improve the quality of life, and I want to help get rid of drugs."

4. What are the main areas in which you will fulfill your purpose? For example, "My focus is on the community, my home, my workplace, and the whole world."

5. Now take your answers to questions 1, 2, 3, and 4 and combine what you think are the most important elements of them to make a complete sentence, as in the following example:

"My purpose in life is"
(write in here your answer to question 1)
"to use my sense of humor, my creativity and my caring for people,"
(write in here your answer to question 2)
"by creating fun projects,"

---

*Adapted with permission from the work of Arnold Patent (1987).

(write in here your answer to question 3)
"that help get rid of drugs,"
(write in here your answer to question 4)
"in my community."

So a first draft of your purpose statement could be *"My purpose in life is to use my sense of humor, my creativity, and my caring for people, by creating fun projects that help get rid of drugs in my community."*

It's important that you state your purpose in the present tense because that way it is always current. You'll most likely discover that you already have been living out your purpose for many years and that the choices you have made throughout your life have usually supported it. It does help, particularly during times of change, to have it at the forefront of your mind so that the ups and downs of the transition curve make more sense and are less able to knock you off balance. Not only does this help keep you healthy, it also helps you see your growth opportunities throughout the change.

You may have more than one purpose in your life, of course. Repeat the exercise as often as you wish to accommodate your *main* purposes. Be sure to record and date each purpose statement in your transition journal.

18

TEN STEPS FOR LIVING WITH CHANGES

This chapter is a handy summary of ideas that will help and support your journey through the changes of your life.

1. *Be Patient With Yourself.* The temptation is almost always to get a transition over with as quickly as possible — and it never seems to work. The seven stages need to be completed, so you will have to be gentle with yourself. There is something of value to be learned in each stage. You'll move fastest if you don't rush. Much gets stirred up during a transition — emotions, behaviors, relationships, lifestyle — and needs to settle. As with those glass or plastic bubbles with "snow" scenes inside — the more it is shaken, the longer it takes to settle. Take it easy.

2. *Don't Be Afraid To Reach Out.* There are many ways you can get help as you move through big changes. Sometimes, you'll just need someone to listen to you. At other times, you may need some professional help; someone to give you a push; someone to provide moral support; someone to go through it with you; or someone who will hold and love you unconditionally. Ask for the support of others when you need it.

3. *Look Forward.* There's always a desire to hold on to at least part of the "old" situation. For a while this is okay, but be careful not to get stuck in the memories. Be clear what you want after "it" is all over, but don't rush the grieving. Both are important. As you move through the transition, find some support and create some continuity in your life. This could be therapy, friendships, hobbies and/or other activities that keep you feeling positive and optimistic about the future.

4. *Stay Open-Minded.* Whatever happens, hold on to your desire to find creative new approaches to old situations. There's always a temptation to stick to old patterns, which may mean that you miss opportunities for new learning. If your transition has been "dropped on you," see if you can find the benefits or opportunities that might come with it. If your transition is one you chose, don't be too surprised if you come face to face with some unexpected emotional hiccups.

5. *Be Good To Yourself.* There's no need play it "tough" during a transition. Spoil yourself, watch your favorite TV shows, take walks, listen to good music, and let yourself go from time to time. Don't be afraid to cry; you'll feel so much better than if you try to keep it all shut up inside.

6. *Go For Walks.* There's always so much more to see and so many different ways to get in touch with the deeper parts

of being human. Spending time outside, watching the changing seasons, playing in the park, being at the shore, climbing mountains, enjoying a sunrise or sunset. Walking leads to many gifts; take time to be alone with nature.

7. *Create Small Successes.* Every success will help you move forward. One of the best ways to move ahead whenever you feel stuck is to create for yourself a small project which you know you'll complete successfully.

8. *Take Some Risks.* It's a great time to try something new. Since you're in transition anyway, why not have a little adventure and do something for the first time? Everything's changing, so why not?

9. *Dream A Little.* The self-fulfilling prophecy is alive and well; "If you can dream it you can do it!" Imagine you have a magic wand and can make the very best of this change. Dream up your perfect outcome and when the dark days creep in *remember the dream.*

10. *Celebrate.* Every ending is also a new beginning. It is important to celebrate both the ending and the beginning. Plan a trip or a retreat for yourself that will symbolize the passage of your transition.

Journey safely!

TOM'S SURPRISE

Tom had expected to work for at least another ten years, but the company he was working with decided they had to go through some major cutbacks, and that meant jobs would be lost. For a couple of weeks, rumors spread like wildfire, and nobody was really sure who would stay and who would go. It was a Friday afternoon when Tom was called into his boss's office to be told that there would no longer be a job for him in the new organization.

Tom tells his reaction:

"I didn't say a word. I just sat there in silence. What could I say? When I left his room, I went straight out into the parking lot and got into my car. I didn't know where I was going, I just wanted to drive around. I didn't want to go home because I didn't know how or what to tell my wife. I parked by the river and sat for about three hours, just staring into space.

"I got home at my usual time, and Sandy, my wife, arrived a little while later. She had always worked, except for a year or two when our kids were infants. But I had always believed that I was responsible for our financial security and thought she'd find it hard to accept that I no longer had a job. (I learned differently later.) So, I waited for the right moment, but she was in such a good mood I didn't want to upset her, and thought I'd wait until we were in bed. I ran out of courage and put it off again. But the next morning, decided to wait until Monday evening, just in case they'd changed their minds at work.

"I'm told I behaved very strangely for the rest of the weekend. I got up several times during the night and was talking in my sleep. I woke up unusually early and cleaned the car — even though it wasn't dirty! I did all the odd jobs I hadn't done for years, and I almost put my shoes in the refrigerator! I think I was in a trance. It is really quite funny now when I look back at it, but it was a weird experience at the time.

"When I went to work on Monday, I felt as if people were looking at me to see how I'd react, but they didn't get any satisfaction because I was the same as ever. It wasn't going to come to anything. After all, I'd been working there for twenty years. When I saw my boss he asked me how Sandy had taken the news, and I remember saying, 'Fine, just fine.' As the day went on, it began to sink in that it wasn't a mistake, I really was going to be without a job in eight weeks.

"Sandy had hardly walked in the door that evening when I told her. After talking very sensibly for a few minutes, we both held onto each other and started to cry. I think it was more the shock of it all than anything else. After all, if you've worked hard and done well for all those years, you don't expect to be told you don't have a job anymore. It's okay if you choose to retire but when you're 'forced' to, it's a whole different ball game.

"It was three weeks before it really hit me that I had to decide whether to find another job or just to retire. Growing up I had received so many messages that I had to be the 'breadwinner' that it was hard to think of retiring at all — much less at my age, for God's sake! I started to get really frustrated with the people I worked with. As for the company ... so that's how they reward people who were loyal to them! As I got angrier, I got more confused about what I really wanted. I started hearing stories of other men who had committed suicide rather than face the prospect of not having a job. Others had hit the bottle or left their families. I could understand all of it. After all, nobody at work seemed to care; as far as they were concerned you were supposed to get on with your job as if nothing had happened. Nobody prepares you for this.

"Sandy and I didn't talk about 'it' much in those early weeks. Except for that moment of weakness, I had kept my control and hadn't told her what was going on inside. She tried to talk to me, but I'd just say everything was fine and change the subject. I suppose I should have talked to her more, but I had too much pride and it got in the way; I thought I was doing everything right. Then, without warning, she let me have it, both barrels! Who did I think I was not to involve her, going it alone? It affected her life, too, and we either were in it together or she was going to go her way and I could go mine. She was so mad that it woke me up to what I'd been doing. I had seen it as my problem, not ours. I think that if she hadn't lost her cool that day I'd have probably been on my own!

"Once the air had cleared and I got the message, we started to talk about some of the alternatives. We found a counselor who worked with people in our situation, and she helped us think about the options. I began to get quite excited about the future and decided that I really wasn't in a hurry to start another job and we had enough money to take a year off at least. In fact, if I was honest with myself I really could retire forever. But it's hard to accept that you're old enough not to have to work again, especially when you think of yourself as still having so much more to give.

"I went to work that last morning still not really believing that I wouldn't be going back. It takes a lot of time to change a twenty-year habit. It's like you *know,* but you don't want to accept it. Sandy had been able to arrange three months off from her job and we hired a motor home and drove to Alaska. It was the best vacation of my life — retirement wasn't all bad!

"When I got home I met up with my buddies and told theall that they should retire, it was great and they must be dumb wanting to continue to work. I think they were upset with me. The atmosphere in the company had changed since the layoffs, and they felt insecure, not knowing what the future might bring. And there I was, sounding off about the joys of retirement, not even bothering to listen to them.

I can see how everything I went through was important, but it was pretty terrible at the time. I began to spend much more time with the garden; I get a lot of pleasure from working with my hands in the earth. It felt peaceful and comforted me when things were crazy. There were times when I wanted to camp out in the yard and only go indoors when I had to. I would go for long walks and sometimes took my fishing rod to the nearby lake. I didn't really care about catching a fish. It was a good excuse to relax and let my thoughts wander. I learned a lot about living from watching nature and realized how much more to life there is than I ever believed in the past.

"After a few more months of not being sure of what to do with myself, I started to think about everything I'd been through and how difficult it had been to let go of all those old habits. I became much wiser as a result of all the pain and confusion, but there had been nobody to turn to, to talk about all the questions and mixed feelings I had. Sandy was great, but she couldn't fully understand. There really is a need for people who can help those who face leaving the work force." So I decided to become a 'Retirement Counselor.' I went back to school for some special training and I feel I'm doing something very worthwhile. I'm happier now than I've ever been, and I'm my own boss, so I take on as much as I want, and have vacations when Sandy and I need to get away. I wouldn't trade places with anyone."

LIFE'S JOURNEY*

I'm quieter now, more peaceful,
I've found a way of living;
not in sacrificing self,
the beauty is in giving.

It's hard to make the change,
to undergo such pain;
but once you realize who you are,
your life will be your gain.

There may be many questions,
with answers hard to find;
but time will give us reason,
and we'll feel peace of mind.

We're here to journey somewhere,
on a road with no direction;
but we'll find courage to proceed,
with love as our protection.

Nature is our comforter,
not position, state or power.
We'll see a world of color
in a tree, a bird, a flower.

Our friends we'll find in truth,
not in acting out a part;
but in trusting and believing
the feelings in our heart.

We're people with a purpose,
to make the world a happier place;
irrespective of our age or creed,
our color or our race.

It's life that is our gift,
we don't see it as our right;
our search will be in sunshine,
now we've travelled through the night.

We'll sail the seas forever,
climb mountains old and new;
and when the darkness falls again,
our strength will see us through.

*Sabina A. Spencer. *Reflections*. New York: Vantage Press, 1987.

REFERENCES

Adams, John D. *Understanding and Managing Stress: Instruments to Assess Your Life Style.* San Diego: University Associates, 1989.

Adams, John D., Hayes, John and Hopson, Barrie. *Transition: Understanding and Managing Personal Change.* London: Martin Robertson, 1976. (New York: Universe Books, 1977.)

Adams, Richard. *Watership Down.* New York: Avon Books, 1975.

Ainsworth-Land, George. Public Lecture. Rhinebeck, NY: The Omega Institute for Holistic Studies. August 4, 1985.

Alberti, Robert E., and Emmons, Michael L. *Your Perfect Right: A Guide to Assertive Living* (6th Edition). San Luis Obispo, CA: Impact Publishers, Inc., 1990.

Bach, Richard. *Jonathon Livingston Seagull.* New York: Avon Books, 1970.

Bach, Richard. *Illusions.* New York: The Bantam Doubleday Dell Publishing Group, Inc., 1977.

Benson, Herbert. *The Relaxation Response.* New York: William Morrow, 1975.

Bridges, William. *Transitions.* Reading, MA: Addison-Wesley Publishing Company, Inc., 1980.

Cooper, Kenneth H. *The Aerobic Program for Total Well-Being.* New York: Bantam Books, 1983.

Fritz, Robert. Public Lecture. Boston, MA: DMA, Inc., March 29, 1985.

Hearst, N., Newman, T.B., and Huller, S.B. "Delayed effect of the military draft on mortality: a randomized natural experiment." *New England Journal of Medicine,* 1986.

Kulka, R.A., et.al. *National Vietnam Veterans Study*. Research
    Triangle Park, NC: Research Triangle Institute, July 1988.
Levinson, Daniel, et.al. *The Seasons of a Man's Life*. New
    York: Alfred A. Knopf, 1987.
NCHS Monthly Vital Statistics Report. September, 1988.
    Hyattsville, MD: National Center for Health Statistics.
Parkes, Colin Murray. *Bereavement: Studies of Grief in Adult
    Life*. London: Tavistock Publications, 1972. (New York: In
    ternational Universities Press, 1972.)
Patent, Arnold M. *You Can Have It All*. Piermont, NY: Celebra-
    tion Publishing, 1987.
Sheehy, Gail. *Passages: Predictable Passages of Adult Life*.
    New York: E.P. Dutton & Co., 1976.
Spencer, Sabina A. *Reflections*. New York: Vantage Press,
    1987.
Tolkein, J. R. R. *Lord of the Rings*. Boston: Houghton Mifflin
    Company, 1955.
Tolkein, J. R. R. *The Hobbit,* or, *There and Back Again*. Boston:
    Houghton Mifflin Company, 1966.

APPENDIX A

FOOD FOR THOUGHT

WRITTEN RESOURCES FOR YOUR JOURNEY

We want you to have a collection of resources which can support and nourish you while you journey. We both have found a great deal of comfort and stimulation from the reading material listed on these pages. This is by no means an exhaustive list. Our intention is to provide you with some of our favorites and to give you a guide to other resources which "speak the same language" and which value the opportunities and challenges that personal change has to offer.

MIND: UNDERSTANDING TRANSITION AND PERSONAL CHANGE

Adams, John D., John Hayes and Barrie Hopson. *Transition: Understanding and Managing Personal Change*. London: Martin Roberston, 1976. (New York: Universe Books 1977.)

Bridges, William. *Transitions*. Reading, MA: Addison-Wesley Publishing Company, Inc., 1980.

Erikson, Erik H. *Childhood and Society*. New York: W.W. Norton and Co., 1963.

Lauer, Robert H. and Jeanette C. Lauer. *Watersheds: Master ing Life's Unpredictable Crises*. New York: Ivy Books/ Ballantine Books, 1988.

Levinson, Daniel, et. al. *The Seasons of a Man's Life*. New York: Alfred A. Knopf, 1978.

Peters, Tom. *Thriving on Chaos*. New York: Alfred A. Knopf, 1987.

Stearns, Ann Kaiser. *Coming Back: Rebuilding Lives After Crisis and Loss*. New York: Ballantine Books, 1988.

Woodward, Harry and Steve Buchholz. *After-Shock: Helping People Through Corporate Change*. New York: John Wiley & Sons, Inc., 1987.

MIND: BELIEFS AND OUTLOOK

Fritz, Robert. *The Path of Least Resistance*. New York: Fawcett Columbine/Ballantine Books, 1989.

Gawain, Shakti. *Creative Visualization*. New York: Bantam New Age Books, Inc., 1982.

Gawain, Shakti. *Living in the Light*. Mill Valley, CA: Whatever Publishing, Inc., 1986.

Harman, Willis. *Global Mind Change*. Indianapolis: Knowledge Systems, Inc., 1988.

Harman, Willis, and Howard Rheingold. *Higher Creativity*. Los Angeles: Jeremy P. Tarcher, Inc., 1984.

Roberts, Jane. *The Nature of Personality Reality*. New York: Bantam Books, 1988.

BODY (Physical Well-Being)

Adams, John D. *Understanding and Managing Stress*. San Diego: University Associates, Inc., 1980.

Bland, Jeffrey. *Nutraerobics*. San Francisco: Harper and Row, Publishers, 1985.

Chopra, Deepak. *Creating Health*. Boston: Houghton Mifflin Company, 1987.

Cooper, Kenneth. *The Aerobics Program for Total Well-Being*. New York: Bantam Books, 1983.

Dossey, Larry. *Beyond Illness*. Boston: New Science Library, 1984.

Eliot, Robert and Dennis Breo. *Is It Worth Dying For?* New York: Bantam Books, 1987.

Friedman, Meyer, and Ray Rosenman. *Type A Behavior and Your Heart*. New York: Alfred A. Knopf, 1974.

Robbins, John. *Diet for a New America*. Walpole, NH: Stillpoint Publishing, 1987.

SPIRIT

Bolen, Jean Shinoda. *Goddesses in Everywoman*. New York: Harper Colophon Books, 1985.

Bolen, Jean Shinoda. *Gods in Everyman*. New York: Harper and Row, Publishers, 1989.

Carey, Ken. *Return of the Bird Tribes*. Kansas City, MO: Uni*Sun, 1988.

Harner, Michael. *The Way of the Shaman*. New York: Bantam New Age Books, 1982.

Marks, Linda. *Living With Vision*. Indianapolis: Knowledge Systems, Inc., 1989.

Monroe, Robert A. *Journeys out of the Body*. Garden City, NY: Anchor Press/Doubleday, 1973.

Neihardt, John G. *Black Elk Speaks*. New York: Washington Square Press/Pocket Books/Simon & Schuster, 1979.

Paulus, Trina. *Hope for the Flowers*. New York: Paulist Press, 1972.

Spencer, Sabina A. *Reflections*. New York: Vantage Press, 1987.

Wright, Machaelle S. *Behaving as if the God in All Things Mattered*. Jeffersonton, VA: Perelandra, 1987.

EMOTIONS

Alberti, Robert E. and Michael L. Emmons. *Your Perfect Right: A Guide to Assertive Living* (Sixth Edition). San Luis Obispo, CA: Impact Publishers, 1990.

Brooks, Anne M. *The Grieving Time*. New York: Harmony Books/Crown Publishers, Inc., 1985.

Ellis, Albert. *How to Stubbornly Refuse to Make Yourself Miserable about Anything — Yes Anything!* New York: Lyle Stuart, 1988.

Jampolsky, Gerald. *Love is Letting Go of Fear*. New York: Bantam Books, 1983.

Jampolsky, Gerald. *Teach Only Love*. New York: Bantam Books, 1983.

Lerner, Harriet Goldhor. *The Dance of Intimacy*. New York:
  Harper and Row, Publishers, 1989.
Tavris, Carol. *Anger: The Misunderstood Emotion*. New York:
  Touchstone / Simon & Schuster, Inc., 1982.

SUPPORT
Bach, Richard, *The Bridge Across Forever*. New York: William
  Morrow and Co., 1984.
Bloomfield, Harold, and Sirah Vettese. *Lifemates: The Love
  Fitness Program for a Lasting Relationship*. New York: New
  American Library, 1989.
Campbell, Susan M. *The Couple's Journey*. San Luis Obispo,
  CA: Impact Publishers, 1980.
Fisher, Bruce. *Rebuilding: When Your Relationship Ends*. San
  Luis Obispo, CA: Impact Publishers, 1981.
Hayes, Jody. *Smart Love*. Los Angeles: Jeremy P. Tarcher, Inc.,
  1989.

APPENDIX B

RESOURCES FOR THE BODY

People going through personal transitions sometimes have little or no interest in food, or begin to eat a diet that lacks important nutrients and contains some not-so-healthy excesses. Such changes in eating patterns may leave them unhealthy and/or cause large weight gains or losses — not a good idea when you're under stress.

Nutrition experts disagree on a lot of things, but most agree that people in the U.S.A. eat a pretty unbalanced diet, overdoing fat, salt, and sugar, and skimping on fruits, vegetables, grains, nuts, and dietary fiber. As a nation, we even consume more protein than we need (although many people don't get enough.) The average U.S. diet is also low in the B and C vitamins — needed for many essential functions in the body, and burned up rapidly during stressful times.

Food itself can be a *source* of stress. Every week there's a new message about what's "good for us," and lots of folks are constantly pursuing the "perfect diet" which will allow them to eat everything in sight and lose weight!

During stressful periods, alcohol, caffeine, tobacco and sugar are, unfortunately, often used more. Each of these substances diverts or destroys the B and C vitamins. If you are not eating more carefully than do most folks, it's likely that you aren't getting enough of these basic nutrients to keep you in good health while you adjust to an important life change.

It's not our goal to create *more* stress for you here by prescribing a "diet." Still, there are some sensible things you can do to improve your eating habits — and thus your well-being — during a life change. The meal ideas offered here are included to help you make some healthy choices. While meals

187

such as these are always a good idea, they are especially important during times of personal transition or other life stresses. You may choose to use these suggested meals as models for developing an eating plan for yourself. Some of our workshop participants find this to be both enjoyable and health-promoting. The combinations suggested below contain a wide variety of "stress-fighting" nutrients, and are reasonably well-balanced.

We hope these ideas will appeal to you, and will be useful additions or substitutions to your "normal" menu.

BREAKFAST IDEAS:

Don't skip breakfast! If you're concerned about getting too many calories, eat less later in the day.

TRY: Sugar-free granola or muesli or hot oat meal or oat bran, with skim or low-fat milk or low fat yogurt
 OR
Oat/wheat bran muffin
 OR
Whole wheat blueberry or raisin pancakes
(NOTE: *real* maple syrup is a complex carbohydrate)
 OR
One or two (maximum) poached or boiled eggs with whole wheat toast with small amount of butter
WITH: Fresh fruit or small glass of fresh or frozen fruit juice
Glass of skim or low-fat milk
Water process decaffeinated coffee, herbal teas, or one cup of caffeinated coffee or tea (but no more than three 5-oz. cups of caffeinated beverages per day)

LUNCH IDEAS:
TRY: Chicken breast teriyaki

Brown rice, Steamed vegetables
> OR

Low-sodium cream of tomato soup
Spinach and whole wheat pasta salad with chicken
  chunks (made with light mayonnaise)
> OR

Steamed jumbo shrimp
Boiled red skin potatoes
> OR

Clear low-sodium vegetable soup
Sliced turkey breast sandwiches on whole wheat bread
  with lettuce, tomato and light mayonnaise
WITH: Whole wheat rolls
Fresh fruit (berries, melon slices, orange, apricots...)
Skim or low-fat milk, mineral water, water process
  decaffeinated coffee, herbal teas, or one cup of caf
  feinated coffee or tea

DINNER IDEAS:

TRY: Clear low-sodium vegetable soup
Poached, broiled or baked white fish — halibut, cod,
  shark, haddock, bass, — with lemon juice
Brown and wild rice or baked potato
Steamed cauliflower
> OR

Low-sodium barley soup
Stir-fried chicken breast with diced vegetables (using
  peanut or canola oil)
Brown rice, Steamed green beans and almonds
> OR

Low sodium chicken with rice soup
Filet of sole (poached or sauteed in olive oil)
Steamed parsley potatoes and vegetables
> OR

Minestrone soup

Roast turkey breast with brown rice and nut dressing
Steamed broccoli or carrots
WITH: Salad with low-fat dressing (may include low-fat
cottege cheese)
Whole wheat rolls
Fresh fruit and yogurt (blend and chill), or sugar-free
gelatin dessert, or low-fat frozen yogurt, or ice milk
Skim or low-fat milk, mineral water, water process
decaffeinated coffee, herbal teas, or one cup of caf-
feinated coffee or tea

A meal plan such as this one is lower in fat, salt and sugar
than the average American diet; moderate in protein; and
high in complex carbohydrates — in other words, it is relatively balanced. What you'll find missing here, compared with
the average U.S. diet, are red meats (high in fats unless
carefully trimmed), fried foods (high in fats), and sugary
desserts. These suggested meals can still have plenty of
calories, however; you will need to consume small-sized por-
tions if you are concerned about gaining weight. (An average
120-pound female needs about 1800 calories per day, and an
average 160-pound male needs about 2400 calories per day,
to maintain their weight.)

If these suggested menus seem strange to you, it is likely
that your present diet isn't well-balanced. Once you become
used to meals like these, try some experimenting; you'll find
a remarkable number of ethnic (Indian, Chinese, Ethiopian,
Mexican, Italian,...) and vegetarian meals which can be
prepared which are low in fats, salt and sugar and high in
complex carbohydrates and fiber.

One last note about food: whatever you eat, make eating
a non-stressful, leisurely activity. Sit down, relax, take time
to savor your food. *How* you eat is not quite as important as
what you eat, but it does matter. Enjoy!

INDEX

... more books with "IMPACT"